$\mathcal{P}$resented to:
Butler Area Public Library

In Memory Of

Jason Ritzert

by

Tri-State Country Music
Association Chapter #3

Hunting Trophy Deer

The Best of *Buckmasters Whitetail Magazine*

Hunting Trophy Deer

The Best of
Buckmasters Whitetail Magazine

Edited by the editors of
Buckmasters Whitetail Magazine

Introduction by Jackie Bushman

The Lyons Press
Guilford, Connecticut
An imprint of The Globe Pequot Press

PERMISSIONS ACKNOWLEDGMENTS

"The 'What If' Buck" by Jackie Bushman
"All-Day Deer Stands" by Scott Bestul
"Silence of the Limbs" by Patrick Meitin
"Deep-Freeze Deer" by Tom Fuller
"Tabletop Scouting" by Tim Rutledge
"Tracking Wounded Deer" by Joel S. Fawcett
"Small Details for Big Farmland Bucks" by Jim Hole, Jr.
"Still-Hunting" by Barry Wensel
"Going to the Boneyard" by John Trout, Jr.
"The Science of Hunting Points" by Brad Herndon
"Forget About Scrapes" by Bill Winke
"Triple Your Deer Harvest" by Charles Pittman
"Ten Tips for Black Powder Hunting Success" by Sam Fadala
"Bow Tuning Made Easy" by Chuck Adams
"Offbeat Tactics for Big Bucks" by Bryce M. Towsley
"Scrape Pattern Know-How" by Kathy Etling
"Sold on Swamps" by Kathy Etling
"The Art and Science of Preparing Venison" by Dave Henderson
"The Tools of Time" by Tim Wells
"The Rattler's Almanac" by Gary Clancy

The Lyons Press is an imprint of The Globe Pequot Press.

Printed in the United States of America

Designed by Compset, Inc.

10 9 8 7 6 5 4 3 2 1

Library of Congress Cataloging-in-Publication Data on file.

Contents

Introduction

I relish the days when I can go hunting or just spend time in the outdoors. Like other hunters, I am in love with the outdoors. That's the bottom line. I fell in love with the outdoors before I was school age. I'm still madly in love with it and the older I get the more I appreciate it. I always come home from a day in the woods feeling refreshed. And, on every trip, I learn something. Sometimes, it's something really significant. Other times, it's just a little snippet of knowledge, but it's that sense of invigoration and the continual wonder of discovery that makes hunting more and more rewarding over the years.

I designed *Buckmasters Whitetail Magazine* to give our readers similar feelings when they finished reading each issue. I want it to trigger that same feeling of renewal. And, when they put each issue down, I want our readers to have learned something that will make them better outdoorsmen, regardless of whether they are beginning, intermediate, or advanced hunters.

We also make it a policy to listen to our readers. As the years have gone by, their desires have dictated what goes into the magazine. We were not the first deer hunting magazine on the market, but we've become Number One by listening to what hunters want. One of our goals is to stay on the cutting edge of information.

I rely on Buckmasters executive editor Russell Thornberry and, more recently, also his son, managing editor Darren Thornberry, to find good writers and good stories with lots of photos. They've done a great job and deserve much of the credit for the success of the magazine. Along the way, they've discovered some good writers among our ranks of readers and have helped them develop their writing careers.

In this book, I've asked Russell and Darren to pick the best how-to stories that have appeared in Buckmasters over the years and they have done their usual masterful job. I hope "Hunting Trophy Deer: The Best of *Buckmasters Whitetail Magazine*" will leave you with that feeling of refreshment that comes from spending time in the outdoors. And I hope you pick up some tips that will help you get that dream buck.

Jackie Bushman

Dedication

When Buckmasters was still young and struggling, I hired several people who helped me get it over the early hurdles. They continue to help make the company a growing success. They are Lewis Figh, Alan Brewer, Dockery Austin, and Russell Thornberry.

Lewis, who is president of Buckmasters, put his accounting shoulder to the wheel and has always made sure the company's books are balanced and the bills paid. He is invaluable in the day to day management of the company. Alan, who is senior vice president, is in charge of our events and has kept the Buckmasters Expo, the Buckmasters Classic, and the Buckmasters Top Bow Indoor competitions running smoothly. It is a monumental job which he makes look easy. Dockery, who is vice president of marketing and head of our Buckmasters Young Bucks Outdoors program, taught us the basics and fine points of putting a magazine together. It was her art, design, and sometimes her writing skills that gave *Buckmasters Whitetail Magazine* its professional look. Russell Thornberry, vice president and executive editor of all our magazines, worked from Canada, and then Texas, before moving to Montgomery and joining us in-house in 1996. His extensive experience as a hunter, guide, and writer have been invaluable.

It is altogether fitting and appropriate that this book be dedicated to four of the best of Buckmasters, Ltd.

Hunting Trophy Deer

The Best of
Buckmasters Whitetail Magazine

1

The "What If" Buck

By Jackie Bushman
(January/February 1989)

What if I hadn't booked this Alberta hunt? What if I hadn't adjusted my scope? What if Russell and I had not been at camp when Will and his guide Sharky came back for help? What if Russell had not glassed the mountain one more time? What if we had not gone down to Harrison Point? What if the buck had gone a hundred different directions instead of toward my stand? The answers to all these questions tell the story of a whitetail hunt I will never forget.

On January 26, 1987, at the Buckmasters Classic, I met one of our invited deer hunting experts, Russell Thornberry of Alberta, Canada. Russell had a reputation for putting deer hunters on some of the world's largest whitetails. It was not until late one night at the Classic that it all sank in. As everybody at the Classic brought out their pictures of big bucks and were telling all those terrible lies, Russell sat quietly eating his dinner, minding his own business. Classic Director and longtime hunting companion Alan

1

Jackie Bushman with the "What If" buck—now the logo buck for Buckmasters.
Credit: Russell Thornberry

Brewer approached Russell and asked him how his past deer hunting season had gone.

He looked up and said, "I thought we had a great year. Out of all of our hunters, we averaged 160 points on all whitetail bucks taken."

When we heard that, Alan and I looked at each other in total shock. "Let me get my scrapbook and show you," Thornberry said, as he got up from the table. When he returned with his scrapbook, any doubts quickly disappeared as we thumbed through this dream book of whitetails. I had never seen bucks with body size or antlers like that before. I looked around, and saw that Alan had his checkbook out. "What are you doing?" I asked. "I don't know about you, but I'm going with Russell this fall," he said, as he wrote out his deposit for the hunt.

Since Alan and I have hunted together for more than ten years, I just couldn't let him go by himself, so I committed, too. With the events that followed, I would have to say this was one of my greatest decisions in life.

The summer flew by, and before we knew it, November was upon us, and it was time to get ready for the hunt. This was a job in itself. I had had a miserable experience in Manitoba the previous fall, practically freeezing to death in – 40-degree weather, and I wasn't going to let that happen again.

Packing enough warm clothes for this year's trip was number one on my list. I was still cramming wool socks into my bag when Alan pulled up to the house to begin our trip. We quickly loaded the truck and were off to the airport, where five bellmen helped us unload our bags and equipment. As we checked in and boarded the flight, we were just hours away from a very eventful week

When the plane touched down in Edmonton, Alberta, we were greeted by Dave, one of our guides. On our two-hour drive to camp, we bombarded Dave with questions. Alberta was having really terrible weather this year. When I say terrible weather for Alberta, I'm talking no snow, and temperatures in the 50s and 60s. Fortunately for us, they had had six inches of snow the night before we arrived. As we learned, hunting whitetails in Alberta with no snow is like finding a needle in a haystack. But snow and cold temperatures are just what you need to kick off the major portion of the rut.

Our anticipation grew as we headed into camp. We were warmly greeted by Russell and his lovely wife, Sharleen, as we walked into the little green cabin. Russell's other top-notch guides—Propane Shane, Bob, Ron, and Sharky—all gave us a very warm greeting. Our hunting companions for the week were Texans Hershel Chadick, Wayne Falcone, and Mike Szydlik, along with Louisianian Will Gray, and Dale Peterson from Pennsylvania.

We put our gear into our rooms and then headed to the rifle range. The first thing Russell requires all shooters to do is make sure that their rifle is zeroed in before the opening morning hunt. As we drove through the open stubble fields, we came to the spot where everybody would shoot their rifles.

Our guides put out some boxes with targets on them, and we drove down about 100 yards to take our shots. I was shooting a 7mm which had zeroed in at 300 yards when I left home. I squeezed off five shots that grouped closely, but were about five inches high at 100 yards. This was a tad bit higher than when I was shooting at home.

Some of the guys told me to leave it because it would probably be OK. Then Wayne walked up as I was putting up my gear and said that he thought I needed to bring it down about two inches to be safe for shooting at the intermediate ranges. Shots in Alberta can be anywhere from fifty to 400 yards. I took his advice and lowered it the needed two inches.

Lowering my zero by two inches turned out to be a critical decision, as I would soon discover. We all loaded back into the trucks and headed back to camp for supper.

Sitting in a deer camp listening to the stories and planning the next day's strategy is, for me, one of the best things about deer hunting. It is my way of getting psyched up for the big challenge. The only problem was that this was not a Southern deer camp!

These guys were talking about world-record-book whitetails and how they were going to hunt them. This really blew my mind because this is a hunter's dream, not really a reality. As the guides talked about "book deer," as they called them, I just sat back and listened. Everything mentioned about a buck was relative to the "book." This was the hunting lingo I had to pick up if I were going to fit in.

If I heard the word "book" mentioned once, I heard it more than a hundred times. The other thing that hit both Alan and me was the bag limit of only one whitetail buck. This might not bother a lot of hunters across the country, but it is a culture shock coming from Alabama, where you can take a buck a day for about two months.

Once you see horns in Alabama, the guesswork is over. Not so in Alberta; that is when the work begins. Alan and I were like two college students who had skipped classes all year but were going to cram all night long for the final exam the next day. We wanted to know what to look for in a buck here. Was it spread? What is tine length? What is mass?

Russell's comment to our questions was "these bucks will only give you four seconds to make a decision and get your shot off." He said when you see a buck and it doesn't impress you, or if there is any hesitation in your mind about a particular buck, don't shoot. But, when you see a buck and your eyes get as big as golf balls and your heart comes through your shirt, the moment of destiny has come: pull the trigger! With all this on my mind, I headed for bed. I knew I wouldn't get any sleep, though. I was too excited!

The next morning came early. I felt like I had just closed my eyes when the light came on. As everybody scurried around and got dressed, we grabbed a quick breakfast and were off on our first morning hunt.

Russell and I drove out to the point of a snow-covered ridge that overlooked a beautiful river bottom. As the engine of the truck stopped, Russell said, "Well, this is it. Get the rest of your clothes on and let's go." The sun was beginning to break behind the snowy ridges as we started down toward the river bottom. With all the clothes I had on, I looked like I weighed 400 pounds, but this ole Southern boy wasn't about to get cold this time.

We made our way around the river's edge until we came to a point in the river. This is where my Texas tower stand was placed. The stand was positioned on the other side of the river overlooking an open flat on the other side. The flat was about 150 yards wide and was surrounded by heavy timber on three sides. Russell told me that does often crossed the flat going from timber to timber. When the rut is in full motion, the big bucks will frequently be right behind them.

Once I got in my tower, I loaded my 7mm and pulled my hat over my ears. Russell was set up right below the tower on a stool with rattling horns ready to clash. After sitting about ten minutes, Russell tickled the tines together, very softly. To my right, about fifty yards away, was the heavy timber that bordered the flat. This was the area I focused on.

When Russell increased his meshing of the horns, I heard limbs breaking back in the timber. At first, I really didn't think anything of it; but when I looked down at Russell, he pointed to tell me that a buck was coming our way. When he did that, my heart grew from the size of a tomato to a watermelon in five seconds. Here I was in my stand only ten minutes, and here comes an Alberta buck. Give me a break. At least let me work into this a little slower.

The cracking of the limbs was getting closer and closer to the edge of the timber beside the river. If he was going to show himself, he would be only fifty yards off to my right. Then there was silence for about five minutes. I kept staring in the direction of the timber. Russell picked up the horns and started thrashing the bushes before putting the horns together for about fifteen seconds. Limbs started breaking again, but they were farther upriver and deeper in the timber.

This reminded me of turkey hunting back home; it was like a smart ole gobbler who just wouldn't come closer. This buck was interested, but not enough to show his face. In the distance a shot rang out, then two more followed. Russell whispered up to me that that was someone in our party, and he was going over to see what happened. After he left, I sat there scanning every square inch of the bottom in hope that something might come across. I figured that the farthest part of the flat was about 300 yards before it hit timber.

From there, the timber began to elevate up the steep ridge. As the ridge began to slope up in front of me, there would be open places anywhere from twenty-five to fifty yards wide and long. There was one particular opening I kept looking at that I figured to be about 600 yards away. Every few minutes I would glance up to check things out. Then something caught my eye.

It wasn't there earlier, but at the same time it wasn't moving. I eased up my binoculars and scanned the edge of the open area. My eyes had not deceived me, because I was looking at a beautiful 10-point buck. He just stood motionless, looking down at the timber below. The buck was too far away to shoot, so I tried to judge his rack. His spread was a few inches wider than his ears, which made him over twenty inches. I could count four points on the beams, with two brow tines to go with them. He seemed to have average mass—nothing really heavy that I could judge. The tines were not extremely long, but were very symmetrical. If I had to score him, I would say he was in the 140 class. Finally, he began to move across the opening with his nose to the ground. What a beautiful sight. He also seemed to have good body size. I just couldn't believe how much he stood out in the snow.

We're not much used to snow where I come from. I think I have seen snow three times, and two of those times were on television! To me, that buck looked like a horse with horns as he walked into the timber and out of sight. When I finally climbed back up the ridge to the truck, I told Russell what I saw and where it was. To my amazement, Russell said the opening was about 400 yards instead of the 600 yards I had estimated. Thank God he wasn't a monster, or I would've really been sick.

Russell told me that one of the hunters in camp, Hershel Chadick, had missed a monster. He was eyeball to eyeball with a "book deer" at about fifty yards, but the thumb on his heavy mitten accidentally touched the trigger as he was beginning to fire. As the warning shot went off, the buck bounded off. Before Chadick could compose himself, the buck had put another 150 yards between them. Two more shots were to no avail.

You could see Chadick's sick feeling as we talked at the truck, so it must have been a really big buck. After talking, we loaded up and headed in for lunch. Then it was back to the woods. Russell had picked out a different spot for me for the afternoon hunt. I was going to be hunting on the opposite side of the river from my morning stand. Driving through the wide-open stubble fields, we approached the heavy timber looking over the river bottom.

The truck stopped. "Hop out here and walk to the bottom of the hill. Your stand will be right on the river," Russell said. I grabbed my rifle and clothes and was on my way. As I started down the hill, I knew I was in trouble. What they call hills, I call major mountains. Thinking my journey would be short, it took me more than thirty minutes to reach my stand, and that was going downhill!

I sure was dreading having to go back up that mountain after the hunt. The stand was right in the corner of the stubble field that bordered the river. Crawling under the fence to get to my stand, I noticed a fence post that had been really torn up by a dominant buck. Back home in Alabama, big bucks pick on some pretty big trees, but I had never seen one shred a fence post. The afternoon seemed to pass quickly from up in that big tree. The only wildlife I saw was a group of three coyotes crossing the ice-covered river. When the sun started to set, I searched with more intensity for movement. Then I caught a glimpse of something walking toward me in the stubble field. Looking through my binoculars, I picked up some movement.

What I saw was a nice rack buck walking at a steady pace right toward my stand. With only a side view, I could count five points, so I knew it had to be a 10- or 12-pointer. The buck stopped, then turned his head away from me. His horns were as wide as his ears, giving him about an 18-inch spread. The tines were of good length with pretty good mass. I was excited, but I remembered what Russell had said: "If he doesn't just blow you away by his presence, don't shoot."

This buck was a good buck in anybody's book. He was bigger than anything I had taken or seen, but he was not the Mr. Big I was looking for. The buck walked off, as my first day of hunting came to a close.

I described the buck that I had seen to Russell and his staff after supper that night. They said he would have scored in the 150s, which really bothered me. I like wide spreads in my whitetail bucks, so that is the first thing that I look for. I was informed that a lot of the "book deer" here have no more than 18-inch spreads, but have long tines with heavy mass. Once I heard that, I threw my wide spread theory out the window. The next buck I saw that was a tad bit better than the first two was going to have lead coming his way.

On Tuesday's hunt, I wasn't as fortunate as I was on Monday. I didn't see a deer in the morning or the afternoon. We did get in some intense scouting during the midday hours, however. Russell and I found some fresh scrapes in two different spots. On Monday Russell had kicked snow into both scrape sites, and when we checked them midday Tuesday, both scrapes had been cleaned out and worked. Our strategy was to hunt one site on Wednesday morning and the other Wednesday afternoon.

As Wednesday morning came around, Russell and I were in position around the scrape area. I was about seventy-five yards downwind from the scrape. Russell got about fifty yards behind me, and tried some horn rattling. As luck would have it, we saw nothing that morning. As we headed back to the truck, I couldn't stop thinking about the bucks I had passed up. I wasn't coping well with the decisions I had made so far.

While back at camp catching a bite to eat, Russell's guide Sharky, Will, and Gordy came into the cabin. "Russell, we need some help down at Harrison Point with Will's buck," Sharky said.

Sharky's little truck couldn't make it down the mountain to the river to bring the buck out, so Russell and I loaded up our gear and headed down there in our big truck. Little did I realize that the next few hours were going to be the most dramatic in my young deer hunting career.

Once we had arrived at the top of the ridge, we knew our work had just begun. Locking the hubs in four-wheel drive, we eased down the mountain to Harrison Point.

Harrison Point is a stand named after Phillip Harrison from Texas, who has had good luck year after year in that spot. It sits out on the point of the river overlooking a large open flat, and is a consistent producer of big bucks. Sharky and Will had gutted the deer, but couldn't get it across the river to get the truck. It was a young 10-pointer that Will mistakenly took for a big buck. I could see how he had misjudged it, because the rack looked huge in proportion to its body. Finally, Russell and Sharky got him across the river. We loaded him in the truck and headed back up the mountain.

When we got about three-fourths of the way up, our tires started spinning and we were going nowhere. This meant it was time for the snow chains. By this time it was about 3:15 in the afternoon, which meant we were late for my afternoon stand. With the snow chains on, we climbed the additional part of the mountain. We took the chains off and loaded Will's buck into Sharky's truck. As Sharky and Will drove off, Russell and I were putting our clothes on so we could drive to my stand and start hunting. My stand was about twenty minutes away. As we pulled up to the top of the ridge, Russell said, "Let me see my binoculars so I can glass the other side of the mountain one more time before we leave."

Moving the binoculars from left to right to cover the complete terrain, Russell stopped quickly at one point. "There's a doe coming out of the timber on the other side of the river."

As he continued to glass the doe, his voice raised to high pitch. "Oh my God, what a buck. He's book class. What a monster!"

"Let me look at him for a minute," I pleaded. Finally getting the binoculars fitted to my face, I began to focus on the area Russell described. I picked up the doe as she was looking back over her shoulder to her right. I moved the binoculars a hair to the right, and there stood the king of kings, a book-class whitetail buck.

My hands started trembling and my heart was racing a mile a minute at this spectacular sight. As the buck moved up behind the doe, there was a small four-foot fence that crossed the flat in which they stood. The doe went under the fence as the big buck just watched her. Then, all of a sudden, the buck leaped into the air and went up and over the fence. I will never forget that sight as long as I live. His massive wide rack gleaming in the sunlight and his huge muscular body floating through the air was a sight to behold. When he hit the ground, he almost put his rack on the ground as he swayed his head back and forth, chasing the doe.

Russell slapped me on the arm. "Hey, you want to try for him?" It took about one second for me to make my decision. We quickly grabbed our gear and started down the mountain toward the river. The plan was to set up close to the river so we could see the open flat on the other side. Russell's intentions were to horn-rattle and see if the buck would react.

The buck would have to travel through the heavy timber and into the open flat before I could shoot.

Once we were in position, Russell started clashing the horns and meshing the tines. My anticipation grew larger and larger. The vision of the buck I'd witnessed in the binoculars was very clear. I could envision him sneaking out of the timber in search of our rattling. After going through numerous rattling sequences, however, it became obvious that Mr. Dream Buck wasn't going to show.

"Jackie," Russell said, "the only other chance we have is to go down to the right and back to Harrison Point. Sometimes the does will walk that long stretch of timber and come across the flat."

With the afternoon slipping by, we had nothing to lose, so we moved briskly toward Harrison Point. I really didn't have much confidence as we approached the stand, since we had just been down there, talking and carrying on with Will's buck. Russell helped me up the tower stand and then went back and sat down on his famous log. He looked up at me and said, "Watch toward your left where the timber comes to a point. That is where the deer come out to cross the flat."

Once he said that, I put a death stare on that particular timber. Then, after sitting there for only about five minutes, I saw some movement toward the timber. I raised my rifle and glared through my scope. A doe was running out of the timber and crossing the open flat right in front of me at about 250 yards. I whispered to Russell that it was just a doe, since he could not see because the riverbank blocked his view. As the doe kept coming across the flat, I caught movement coming out of the timber. Picking it up in my scope, I could tell it was a buck.

"Russell, it's a buck, it's a buck!" I whispered loudly. "Can you see him? Can you see him?"

Russell replied, "I can't see a thing. The decision is yours." That's all I needed to hear. All that I could think about was the buck I'd seen in the binoculars. I didn't want to shoot this buck because I felt we might get a chance to hunt the monster buck later in the week. As the buck got closer and closer, I could only see a side view of his rack. It looked like it had good beam length. Russell was saying, "If he's good, take him."

Since I had already passed up two pretty good bucks and this one looked as good as they did, I decided to take him. The buck was moving at a steady pace now, as he was trying to catch up with the doe. The only problem was the buck was in a swell or dip in the open flat. I could only see from the middle of his body to the top of his back.

I took the safety off and placed the crosshairs in the middle of this area. I then moved it all the way to the front of his chest. With the pace he was moving, this was enough lead for me to hit his vital areas. The crack of the 7mm echoed through the river bottom. As I bolted my rifle with another cartridge, I looked back through my scope and was amazed to see that the buck was standing there, looking me eyeball to eyeball in my scope. At that instant, I realized this was the same magnificent buck I had seen in the binoculars!

My heart pounded fiercely as I tried to restore my composure. I just couldn't believe I was staring at a book-class whitetail, much less that I'd just shot and missed, only to have him stand dead still and look at me. With my nerves a little more stable now, I again placed the crosshairs in the middle of the area that was exposed behind the front shoulder. The buck was still in the dip, as he was when I first shot. The second shot went off as the 7mm kicked up in the air. I quickly looked in my scope and saw nothing at the spot where I had shot. Then I saw the buck trying to get up and make his way off.

I aimed one more time and fired as the buck was stumbling off, but saw nothing through the scope. Russell was asking, " Did you get him?" I said I knew I'd hit him, and believed it was the same buck we'd seen.

"Jackie, if you got the same buck we were looking at, you've got one heck of a wall hanger! Come on! We have to cross the river and go find him," Russell said.

"I don't have waders to cross the river," I replied. Russell just looked back at me and said, "This will be the best cold you will ever feel if you got the buck we saw."

As the water went over my boots, I felt cold like I never have felt.

Climbing up the riverbank, I hurried to the spot where I thought the buck was. But there was nothing in sight as I covered the flat. There was no blood and no hair, and I walked all the way toward the timber. By this time, I was beginning to feel sick to my stomach. I couldn't believe I had missed the opportunity of a lifetime.

Russell had swung back to the left from the spot where I thought the deer was while I continued to search. Then he yelled over, "Jackie, come here! I think I've found what you're looking for!" As I approached, I could see it was a buck. Once I was on top of him, I knew it was Mr. Big.

Mr. Big was a beautiful 12-point buck. He was a typical 10-pointer with forked brow tines. His beam length was twenty-five inches with a twenty-one-inch outside spread. His BTR composite and Boone & Crockett gross scores were 174 points. What a beautiful sight it was.

I did notice that I had clipped his backbone on my second shot. As Russell and I jumped up and down, hollering and screaming and giving high-fives in the middle of that open flat, high up in Alberta, Canada, it was a day that could not be put into words. Taking this buck was the same as if I had won Wimbledon during my tennis career. It was more than just a dream—now it was reality.

My friends have always said I was lucky, and sometimes I have to believe them. They say I have a horseshoe stuck in a place where the sun doesn't shine. That's fine with me, because I'll take luck any day of the week over expertise.

When we got my buck back to camp, you would think my week was over, but that didn't seem to be the case. In fact, from a good luck story, we went to a bad luck one.

My hunting companion Alan just couldn't see a nice buck. His first morning, he had a small buck walk right under his stand. Then he sat at Harrison Point for two days and saw nothing. I sat there ten minutes and got Mr. Big. Then he hunted the place where I was supposed to hunt before we had to help Will and Sharky. He rattled in a spike, of all things. To make matters worse, I saw three more big bucks from the truck while waiting on Alan.

Two of these were book deer. One big 10-point made a scrape in a wide-open pasture and then walked up to within thirty yards of the truck and just stared at me while poor Alan was sitting in his stand. That just goes to show that being in the right place at the right time sure makes a difference.

As I look back on this incredible hunt while admiring Mr. Big on my den wall, all those questions stick out in my mind. What if Russell and I had not been in camp when Will and Sharky needed help? What if Russell had not glassed the mountain one more time? What if the buck hadn't come toward Harrison Point? What if Wayne hadn't told me to adjust my scope? Now, as this story comes to an end, you can understand why it was called the "what if" buck.

You might have a "what if" buck in your home area this year. If you do, my horseshoe is not for sale!

2

All-Day Deer Stands

By Scott Bestul
(November 1996)

The Wisconsin firearms season was one day and five hours old and I'd seen only a handful of whitetails. The day before I'd abandoned my traditional, favorite Opening Day Stand to experiment in a new area, and my theories about deer movement in that spot had just plain been wrong. By the time dusk had settled on the opener I'd talked myself back to my familiar upland ridge for the next morning.

The first few hours of Day Two produced a deer sighting or two; not much to crow about in the whitetail-rich woodlands of central Wisconsin. But after looking at my watch, I was confident that things were going to get very, very good in the next few minutes.

The noon whistle had just sounded in the nearest town a half-dozen miles away when I turned to face two well-worn trails running south of my stand. As the last notes of the whistle faded I saw a nice doe picking her way toward me on the closest trail. When she stopped and turned to look

Perhaps the best time to hunt in a stand all day is at the beginning of hunting season, when pressured deer are likely to come by at almost any moment.

Credit: Ricky Jansen

behind her, I did the same, and saw another doe, then a sleek, handsome buck following the lead doe as she wandered toward my tree. The deer milled in the thick cover just out of range for awhile, then suddenly stared down their backtrail, raised their tails slightly, and trotted under my tree. My muzzleloader roared, and the buck remained.

Of course I'd love to assert that I knew those deer were on their way to me for a variety of biological and social reasons—but I'd be lying if I did. What I did know, however, was that the hunters who tromped the parcel of land south of my stand are diehard worshippers of the noon whistle. When that siren sounds twelve bells, they stop whatever they are doing and meet back at the cabin for lunch. Truth be told, it wasn't the first time they'd chased deer to me while making their mad dash for midday groceries. Their behavior isn't unique in our hunting area, and members of our group have discovered that staying in our stands through the middle of the day is one of the best ways to capitalize on this hunter movement. We now consider all-day stand hunts one of our most reliable strategies, especially when hunting pressure keeps deer on the move.

Like most stand hunters, I focus the bulk of my efforts on morning and evening vigils. The whitetail is, after all, a crepuscular critter, and the majority of his movement centers on dawn and dusk activity periods. But whitetails, unlike people, don't center their lives around a watch; they don't *have* to move in the first or last sliver of light we frequently call "prime time." Deer move when they need or want to, and that movement frequently occurs in the mid-morning to early afternoon time slot most of us reserve for scouting or hanging around camp.

I've experienced enough incidents like the one described earlier to convince me that staying in a stand for all legal shooting hours is an excellent tactic in a variety of hunting situations. In fact, I've taken enough, and seen even more, nice bucks in the midday that I often feel guilty when I abandon a stand after a morning sit. I'm not saying that every time I hunt, I expect to see deer throughout the day; but there are some special situations that exist in the whitetail's life that make him a midday mover. When I feel those situations exist, I do my best to stay up a tree all day.

Let's look at some of the events that dictate day-long deer movement, and how to capitalize on them with an all-day stand hunt.

Perhaps the best time to pull an all-day stand hunt is when whitetails are being pressured. The hunt described earlier is a perfect example of this, with neighboring hunters unwittingly pushing deer to me as they gathered for lunch. But noon meals are only one example of this human activity; hunters taking coffee breaks, walking to ward off cold feet, or making social visits are all common behaviors where I hunt, and all activities that keep deer moving.

There are, of course, nearby deer drives executed by hunters to push deer to each other, but frequently move deer to unintended standers. Most of my hunting is done in Minnesota and Wisconsin, where a classic scenario unfolds every year. Members of a group take a stand for the first hour or two, then gather and make drives for the remainder of the day. When this type of hunter behavior exists, you'll actually see some of your best deer movement throughout the midday hours, as whitetails are booted from one patch of cover to another, and move constantly, seeking a safe haven from the pressure.

Selecting a stand site for an all-day sit for pressured deer can be as simple as locating the thickest cover in your hunting area. Remember, whitetails on the lam will almost always seek out cover that makes them feel secure—and for most deer, secure means thick. We focus on dense, brushy habitat such as recent clear-cuts, areas of downed treetops, cedar-covered hillsides, and swamps or marshes. These tangles allow whitetails to capitalize on their best defense: laying low. Walk your hunting area thoroughly, noting wherever you find such security cover. Then determine how deer are entering the tangle, and prepare a stand site that considers prevailing winds and offers good shooting.

The other example of a good stand location for pressured deer is a funnel. Funnels, or bottlenecks, are simply natural or man-made obstacles that channel deer movement through a narrow area. Saddles in a ridge, a line of trees through a swamp, a strip of land between two lakes, a shallow crossing in a deep gully or ravine—all are examples of terrain features that channel deer movement and can be relied on as good stand sites. If the funnel leads to a good bedding or escape cover area, you've just upped your odds considerably!

A second situation that deserves an all-day stand hunt is that magic time just prior to, and during the peak of, the annual rut. As bucks increase their search for receptive does, their roaming frequently has them out and about in the middle of the day. I have too many personal memories of rutting, trophy-class whitetails I've seen from ten o'clock to two to relate here, but perhaps the most memorable occurred in Wisconsin three years ago.

I couldn't hunt that particular morning, but headed out to my stand about 12:30, hoping to catch any early afternoon movement. I was too late, even then. When I snuck into my area, there were a large doe and a buck of Boone and Crockett proportions moving within ten yards of my tree. They spotted me about the same time I saw them, and my hunt was over before it began. Isn't there a saying that goes "I'd rather be an hour early than a minute late"? Brother, I believe it!

This is only one example of a huge-buck-in-the-middle-of-the-day incident that has made me a believer in all-day sits during the rut. While I can't claim the self-discipline to do this too often, I try to pull off several all-dayers when I see rut activity picking up. I locate my stands next to the best buck sign as the rut approaches, then move my stands between bedding and feeding areas of doe groups as breeding activity heats up. Frequently, these areas overlap, but not always. It can be a tough decision to make, but sometimes it's best to abandon buck sign and concentrate your efforts on finding does and their bedding areas—the bucks will show up before too long.

A third example of a good time for an all-day stand hunt is when whitetails are feeding well in midday hours. There are a variety of factors that compel deer to feed when the sun is high, but the strongest in my hunting areas appears to be cold weather. Our archery seasons last until December 31, and when hunting in this "late season," we frequently observe deer up and about in the middle of the day. In fact, I have placed stands for evening hunts in the winter, only to find deer moving *from* their feed *to* their beds just when I thought the opposite would occur. I asked a deer researcher I know about this phenomenon in the winter months. According to Jay, northern range whitetails frequently move in midday hours in order to take advantage of the stronger sun and warmer temps, which helps conserve energy. This behavior is so common in our area that I know of a couple successful archers who don't leave the house on winter hunts until midmorning, sit till mid-afternoon, then head home about the time others are heading out!

There's also a growing body of evidence to show that the moon influences deer behavior, putting them on the move at midday. While I have little experience using these lunar charts to predict deer behavior, there are several well-known hunters who swear by the system. I have no doubt that moon phase and position exert some—and quite possibly a strong—pull on whitetails. It will be interesting to watch as this method of predicting deer movement is studied more thoroughly and understood better over time.

To capitalize on midday deer feeding movement, I locate my stands just slightly off the food source. Sometimes, as in our late season hunts, the stand must be extremely close to the feeding area, as deer may be bedded nearby. It's been my experience that when deep cold settles into our area, deer want to take the shortest, fastest route from bed to breakfast, sometimes bedding within sight of the food source. As you might guess, stand placement is a tricky business in such a situation, and careful consideration must be given to the proper approach to each site, as well as not oversetting the spot. Repeatedly spooking whitetails near feeding areas results in later, shorter, and more nervous visits by deer.

Equipment for the all-day stand hunter is crucial to the tactic's success. I start with my largest, most comfortable tree stand, as nothing pushes me to insanity more quickly than standing on a postage-stamp-sized platform for several hours. A good safety belt is, as always, essential gear; you'd be surprised how easy it is to forget you're airborne after sitting up there half a day. Besides my gun or bow, my most important piece of equipment is my daypack. I seem to fill every nook and pocket with binoculars, rattling horns and call, hand warmers, extra clothing, food and water, and extra gear specific to the season.

I mentioned food and drink on my daypack list, but they deserve special attention from the all-day stand hunter. When I started pulling some day-long sits, I picked the brain of a local exercise physiologist who does a lot of winter camping, asking him what I should bring up my tree with me. His advice was to focus on foods rich in carbohydrates that your body burns slowly and converts into the calories that keep you warm. Granola and GORP (Good Ol' Raisins and Peanuts) are good choices; they're easy to carry, quiet, and tasty. Cold pasta is another fine, though less convenient, option. Fruits such as apricots and apples are also excellent foods, and good for you, too. Avoid so-called "quick energy" foods like candy and chocolate, which give you a warm glow for a while, then let you crash and burn.

Liquids are extremely important for day-long stand hunters, and anyone who hunts frequently in cold weather. It's surprisingly easy to become dehydrated in cooler weather, as you don't notice your body sweating like you do in warmer temps. Consequently, many cool-weather deer hunters reduce their liquid intake to near-zero—a real mistake, according to my physiologist friend. "A well-hydrated body is a warmer body," were his words. His recommendations? "Drink water. Lots of it. If mixing Tang or some drink mix will make you drink more, do it. Avoid coffee and other caffeinated drinks. Caffeine reduces circulation and will make you colder." So drink lots and stay warmer—end of sermon.

An all-day sit can be tough on you mentally, too. Unless the action is fast and furious, or you've got the metabolism of a garden vegetable, you'll fight boredom, fatigue, and resignation at some point. If I catch myself getting antsy, I do one of two things: pull out a paperback from my daypack, or get out of my tree and take a brief walk. I've taken some ribbing about the reading, but I figure it's better than leaving the woods or going stir crazy. The walks are a lifesaver, too. You'd be surprised how good you feel after just five minutes of looking at things from ground level.

If you've guessed that all-day stand hunts are not for the faint of heart (or better yet, mind), you're right. I make it a point not to string too many of them together, and feel I avoid getting burned out or fatigued because of it. But those magic times when a dandy buck or group of does appears at an hour when I'd normally be out of the woods, something wonderful happens. All those lonely, deerless minutes disappear, and I relearn the all-day stand hunter's greatest secret—"Prime Time" is any time that the deer say it is!

3

Silence of the Limbs

By Patrick Meitin
(July 1997)

When dealing with the ever-jumpy whitetail, a silent bow can mean the difference between pinpoint shot placement, a miss, or worst of all, a wounded animal. White-tailed deer are perhaps North America's most tightly wound big-game animals, prone to ducking and jumping arrows shot from even the very fastest cam bows. This is a glaring fact which some bowhunters seem inclined to ignore, judging from some of the riotously buzzing, violently vibrating "hunting" bows I have heard on the target line of the local bowhunter hangout.

One of the largest factors I see today can be directly attributed to the industry's need for more speed, pushing bows to greater limits in an effort to squeeze a few more feet-per-second out of sufficiently quick setups. This means shooting increasingly lighter arrow shafts out of bows cranked for maximum poundage, as well as overdraws, that can begin to approach dry-firing decibel levels. This all can become ridiculous, considering your

A smallish 8-pointer standing in weeds at the edge of a forest. If he's this close, silence is golden for bowhunters. *Credit: Jack Brock*

average white-tailed deer is taken well under twenty-five yards. A quiet bow is infinitely more important to my thinking than blinding arrow speed.

There are many important points to consider and many helpful products readily available to help quiet any whitetail rig, and we will get into these shortly. I think it is important at this point to first address an overall approach to building the whitetail setup—your mindset, let us say. I have already touched on the speed craze and the resulting clamor that can result. I am not saying speed unto itself is a bad thing, but there are reasonable limits, a point of diminishing returns.

Stand hunting, given certain inherent realities like long waits in sometimes bitter cold, resulting in stiff muscles, makes hefty poundage a bad beginning in most situations. Determine what poundage you can comfortably pull during backyard practice, and back off 5 to 10 pounds. This assures that you can draw from your tree stand with teeth chattering and muscles quivering with cold when that big buck presents himself at an odd angle. Combined with arrow shafts of moderate weights, such as 2117, 2216, 2315, or 2317, you have a noise-absorbing setup less likely to alert your quarry at the shot. These stiffer shafts, combined with a heavier, wide-profile broadhead, combine for an arrow which drives deep from steep downward elevated stand angles and leaves a conspicuous blood trail. Many archers would disagree with this philosophy; but sacrificing a bit of speed in the interest of silence makes more sense than trying to overtake, with raw speed, an animal possessing the quickest reflexes on this continent.

Riser Pads

Aside from a relatively conservative setup, there are many more avenues available to the archer to tame a garrulous bow. Beginning in logical sequence, let us concentrate on metallic clicks that can result should your arrow fall from the rest and contact the bow's riser, before the shot or while drawing. The obvious solution is riser pads of moleskin or fleece that muffle these inadvertent mistakes. Many manufacturers offer such material in various camo and color schemes, ready to apply with adhesive backing after being cut to shape with scissors. E.W. Bateman offers pads in every imaginable camo pattern, such as Trebark, Mossy Oak Treestand and Fall Foliage, Browning Mossy Oak, Rancho Safari Trebark, and Four-Season. Others include Kolpin's Solid Brown and Bark Camo, and Saunders' Foam Quiet Cushion in brown. Alaska Bowhunting Supply offers slick seal skin for this purpose. E.W. Bateman and Wyandotte Leather, Inc. offer clipped calf skin. If arts and crafts are not your forte, the Cat-Pad by Rancho Safari, Game Tracker's Whisper Silencing Pad, and an offering by Kolpin come pre-cut to fit the average riser.

This material can also be an important addition to your arrow rest, as it doesn't do to have a wet or dirty arrow squawk like a horsehair bow drawn across a violin string when that big buck shows. Carefully cut small pieces of moleskin, and wrap rest arms so that the material does not interfere with the mechanics of the arm. Plunger buttons or side plates are easily protected by stretching a horizontal strip over the surface, adhered to the riser front and rear.

String Silencers

The string silencer is probably the one bow-dampening device every bowhunter is familiar with, as it is the most universal for this purpose, alleviating the guitar-string-like "twang" upon releasing. These are fashioned from a variety of materials, depending on your tastes, and tied to the string one-third the distance from the bow tip to assure the most efficient string silence while affecting arrow energy to a minimum. I find a half portion of material on each bow harness or cable also makes for a quieter bow. The fact remains that weight added to the string will slow arrow speed, if only slightly.

We are talking a few feet-per-second at best. The degree of consequence is in direct proportion to the weight of the material employed. To this end, yarn is slightly lighter than fleece, fleece lighter than rubber whiskers, whiskers lighter than molded rubber.

The discussion does not end here, though. Yarn puffs pick up burrs and bothersome seeds, as well as being slightly absorbent in wet conditions. Fleece becomes soggy in the rain. Rubber whiskers are completely waterproof, though they will hold a small amount of surface tension water, while molded products will not. You make the decision.

Yarn materials are available from E.W. Bateman, Puffs and Cam Puffs from Saunders, and Game Tracker. These are easily installed by inserting one end of the mounting tag (to which the yarn material is sewed along its length) between the strands of the bow string, winding the yarn into a tight ball, then reinserting the opposite tag end back into the string at a 90-degree angle from the first. Tarantula Legs, by Sportsman's Outdoor

Products, are constructed similarly but make use of long strips of fleece material. Other fleece silencers include wider, flat sections of fleece inserted between string strands, made by Game Tracker and Browning.

Rubber whisker material is installed onto the string by a simple overhand knot, or by carefully winding serving material tightly around the silencers and bow string and tying it off securely. Rancho Safari offers the original Cat Whiskers. Game Tracker offers rounded material. Bohning offers String-Whiskers, while similar products are produced by Kolpin and Saunders. Bohning's whiskers come with quick "zip" fasteners, a great idea to clamp the rubber silencers around the string quickly.

Unique to the sport, and of special interest to traditional shooters, Alaska Bowhunting Supply offers both Qiviut and fur string silencers, the former woven of super-light, naturally water repellent musk oxen under wool, the latter from water-resistant seal or beaver pelt. For the compound shooter, Kolpin's silencing device, the Cable Silencer, snaps to each cable where they cross to cut vibration in this area.

Hunting Stabilizers

The job of the hunting stabilizer is not only to balance and steady the bow while aiming, but to absorb riser vibration after the arrow is released. This is accomplished by dissipating or absorbing wholly the energy that is created by the violent action of a bow through loaded energy to sudden action to complete recovery. Energy is assimilated through materials that cause no noise during recovery, such as rubber bushings, mercury or other such heavy liquids, or disperse this byproduct through mechanical means, such as plungers. Choices abound in both areas.

One of the best noise suppression stabilizers around is Saunders' rubber-mounted Torque Tamer, by far the lightest of the noise-absorbing types. Browning Archery manufactures both fluid and mercury-filled stabilizers, including the Hydrocoil, available in 7- or 11-inch models, and Hunting and Hexagonal Mercury Stabilizers.

Hydraulic or pneumatic stabilizers have become the rage of the sport, and are now available from too many manufacturers to mention all of them. Some of the most well-made come from Golden Key Futura, like the Ace Magnum, Hunter, and Mini-Mag Hydraulic; Satellite's Orion Dissipator, Okie Manufacturing's ShootinCushin, Beman's Diva IBO, Game

Tracker's Hydro-Torq, and Archery Shooting System's Super Shot. Others are made by Hydraflight and Hi-Tek. Outback Industries' Pro-Hydro boosts consistency to minus 50 degrees Fahrenheit, while Xi's Pneumatic allows custom tuning to your own bow.

Troubleshooting and Maintenance

With today's myriad selection of attached bow accessories, it is easy to develop inadvertent hums and rattles, which can be difficult to locate and correct. Bow quivers, sight racks and pins, arrow rests, wrist slings, and overdraws can all become culprits after repeated shooting, or even when first installed. Obviously, the first place to begin when such a droning surfaces is with an allen wrench and pliers in hand, tightening every moving part to be found on your bow and accessories. This should alleviate the problem.

Other solutions to prevent problems before they surface are to add moleskin, additional rubber bushings, or wax to surfaces most likely to create complaint. Begin by adhering moleskin between sight rack mounting plates and the bow riser. To destroy tuning-fork hums emitted by many sight racks, wrap rubber bands around extension bars and unoccupied rack areas. If your arrow quiver does not have dampening foam in its hood, make it so. Adjustment screws in rests, sights, and quivers should receive a good dose of Lok-Tite. Rubber bushings to place between quiver and bow, stabilizer and riser, can be found at hardware stores, or cut from rubber mats or tubing. Wax dovetail mounts to make a tighter fit. Add moleskin or heat-shrink tubing to rest arms, foam at contact points on flipper arms. Add additional set-screws by drilling and tapping threads to rests or overdraw systems that have a tendency to pivot and become loose.

Lubrication is often necessary at axle points, rocker arms, and cable slides for obvious reasons. In relatively dirt-free environments, gun oil or oil-suspended Teflon products like TriFlow work well, especially in damp or salt-air conditions found in the South or along the eastern seaboard. In dust-ridden conditions of early seasons, oil attracts grit that causes wear and grinding or squeaking noise. Look to graphite powders or Teflon sprays with carrying agents which dissolve, leaving only dry powder behind. In extremely frigid conditions, like those found in northern Canada during rut time, it may be necessary to take your bow apart and wipe away all lubricants to avoid gumming and sticking parts. Don't be afraid to disassemble your bow to its component parts periodically, and thoroughly clean each and every part and apply fresh lubricant.

The cable slide of any given bow can be a common troublesome area, the factory slide sticking, rubbing, and often squeaking from wear or exposure to the elements. Add hard car wax to the slide extension to provide a hard, slick surface. An additional option is an aftermarket slide, more carefully constructed to minimize surface friction. One of my favorites is the Speed Slide Cable Saver from Outback Industries, a Teflon-bearing unit that surrounds the slide bar to prevent dirt from accumulating beneath it. Game Tracker's solid Teflon cable slide is similar, but lacks the free-floating pivot system of the Speed Slide. Browning's WhisperGlide and Free Wheel Cable Roller Guides contain small wheels to carry cables silently up and down the slide bar. The Kwik Slide by Saunders is designed much the same way.

String-jumping white-tailed deer should be the rare exception, reserved only for campfire explanations after the occasional missed shot that should not have been. Consistently successful whitetail hunting involves attention to the smallest details, and in these meticulous hair-splittings, a quiet bow is one of the easiest factors within your control. Many friends have accused me of an obsessive nature when it comes to bow silence. If by obsessive they mean excessive, I have to disagree. I have been known to experience fits of tearing bows down suddenly, ferreting out a small squeak or buzz during the middle of a shooting league. But obsessive? There is no such word in the vocabulary of the dedicated whitetail hunter!

4

Deep-Freeze Deer

By Tom Fuller
(December 1994)

The warm glow of our heater belied the cold fury of the season's first good snowstorm outside. I was in northern New England, late in deer season, and I was hunting with an experienced and devoted outdoorsman, Ed Lofland. After spending the day in the raw cold of the slate gray November woods, neither of us was surprised by the worsening weather. Just after supper, the wind had come up in earnest and the snow had started blasting against the side of the camper.

"Better bundle up tomorrow," said Ed. "This one feels like it's going to settle in for a while. And it's going to be cold hunting in the morning."

He was right. When we stepped out into the dim daylight the following morning, there were six inches of snow on the ground, and a strong northeast wind slapped at our faces. Ed pulled on his daypack and adjusted his balaclava over his face. "Those deer," he said, "are going to be holed up tight, either in that thick spruce on the back side of the hill out of the

27

Still-hunting through thick cover produced this monster. *Credit: Tom Fuller*

wind, or down in one of those cedar bogs by the brook. Don't stand too long for them because they won't be moving much. And if you're not back by noon, I'll come looking for you."

I struggled up the hill through the snow and spent more time wiping the snow off of my scope than I did looking for deer. I managed to still-hunt across the hidden spruce grove on the lee side of the hill, and back around and through a pocket of fir on the return trip to camp. But by noon I hadn't seen a deer; I was totally exhausted, and nearly frozen.

When I got back to camp, Ed was just coming out of the pines near our little clearing. He didn't look any better than me as we both stumbled into the warmth of the camper and then shed layers of wool coats, insulated vests, and felt pack hunting shoes. Sitting near the heater with a cup of hot soup in my hands, I was about ready to give up, but Ed, as usual, maintained his exuberance.

"That good buck is still around," he said. "I cut his track today. He's just changed what he's doing now. For us to get a good shot at him, we've got to change, too, and this storm will help. He'll really start feeding once it stops blowing; plus, he's already lost his interest in the does."

We hunted hard again that afternoon, and when I cut my own tracks from the morning, I found that a single deer had followed me for more than 100 yards (literally using the trail that I had blazed) to get into the pocket of fir trees out of the wind. I, in turn, followed his trail down into the heavy cover, but when I found tracks that indicated he had started running hard, I knew he had pinpointed me and was now long gone.

The two days that followed were cold, but the wind had died down, and both Ed and I began to see plenty of sign of feeding, meandering deer. They still stayed in the cover, but it became obvious that the deer were finding high energy under the deep-cover apple trees that are so abundant in the New England woods.

On the second afternoon after the storm, I heard the distant crack of Ed's .308. An hour later, when I got to the area where he said he'd be hunting, I was just in time to help him drag out a fine 8-point buck.

What I learned in those last few days of the season proved that deer *do* change—often drastically as the season progresses—but never more than when the first hard cold of winter settles in. Their priorities change almost completely. The passions of the rut have declined and the realities of the long winter ahead have taken hold. While good bucks will certainly pay attention to any stray does that might not have been bred earlier, they are much more inclined to get away by themselves to try and regain some of the body weight and strength they've spent during the long mating season. They'll find isolated safe havens where they won't be disturbed, and will concentrate on food and rest.

Hunting these bucks requires a different plan from the earlier season, too. The plan must center on knowing where the bucks will go, what feeds they'll be concentrating on, and how they will have responded to the change in the weather and the rigors of both the breeding and hunting seasons.

Hunters hoping to put one of these late-season bucks in their scopes need to be prepared to work harder for them, go farther, and be smarter, because these bucks have survived where many others have not. Hunters must also understand the demands of this more severe weather on both their equipment and their bodies, and they must be prepared to handle the dangerous vagaries of winter weather.

The first problem, of course, is finding the deer. The good buck sign that was the focus earlier in the season now loses much of its meaning. The freshly rubbed saplings that helped define a buck's breeding territory are now largely meaningless, and the impassioned pawings and scrapes on the forest floor have outlived their usefulness. While they may indicate that a good buck is still in the area, he will not pay any particular attention to keeping them fresh or to checking them routinely. Instead, that same buck, while certainly not vacating the area, will shift to thicker cover, make his safety a priority, and look for that small, ideal piece of habitat where he can both rest comfortably and yet feed nearby. Knowing this, a hunter needs to concentrate his efforts on these areas, too.

The key to locating these ideal pieces of cover is understanding that good bucks need both safety and food to keep them happy. And the food they will be concentrating on late in the season will be different from what they were using early on. By the time the cold settles in and the snows (that are bound to stay all winter) have fallen, most of the mast crops are gone. Because they are such a favorite food, acorns, beechnuts, and the like attract deer as soon as they hit the ground. And you can be sure the deer will stay on these mast crops until they are used up.

Later in the year, when the cold and snow arrive in earnest, the deer will go to their next favorite food. In the Northeast, that usually means frozen apples, and the twigs, shoots, and buds that sprout up around wild apple trees. In other areas of the country, white cedar might be the primary food source, and in others, aspen or poplar shoots and twigs.

In each section of the country—indeed, in certain areas of particular regions—deer will naturally gravitate to one particular favorite food. While they are certainly browsing animals and will always eat many kinds of food, one type (whether it be apples, cedar, maple, aspen, or whatever) will form the bulk of their diet. A late season hunter needs to identify that food and concentrate his efforts on where both that food and good cover coexist.

It is also important to note that the places where a deer finds its favorite foods, especially the ones used during the winter, can change from one year to the next. While experienced hunters understand this implicitly, even they can get into the habit of looking for their deer in the same places year after year.

While particular crops (like apples) can have off years, forcing the deer to find other food sources (the places where there are ample favored browse plants) can change, too. Young growth shoots and saplings quickly outgrow their usefulness to deer.

Cedar thickets can show a distinct browse line that won't regenerate for several years. And many productive-looking havens that still provide safe cover may well have outlived their food supply. In short, new safe havens that the good bucks will be using late in the season need to be identified each year.

In addition, the methods that a hunter uses in the good areas that he has identified need to be adapted to this late-season, deep-freeze weather. During the early stages of the season, several factors will usually dictate that standing is the best method for intercepting a good buck. These factors include the rigors of the rut, which will keep both bucks and does up and moving much of the time, and also the presence of other hunters. With more hunters in the woods early in the season, the deer are much more likely to be up and about.

In the freezing temperatures of the post-rut late season, however, deer move around much less. The urge to chase does has waned, and there are fewer and fewer hunters in the woods to disturb a deer's natural tendency to feed and rest. That means that a late-season hunter needs to change his tactics to match what the deer are doing.

Stand-hunting near a concentrated food source may well be the best tactic early and late in the day, but it will only be productive during

A prime time to find big bucks like this is right at the tail end of a major snowstorm. *Credit: Donald M. Jones*

these fringes of daylight. During the middle of the day, still-hunting will produce the most encounters. With the deer now resting during most of the daylight hours, a hunter standing in one spot while his good buck is lying down in another spot is useless.

Yet this late season type of still-hunting needs to be adapted, too. Typical still-hunting earlier in the season sees a hunter moving slowly throughout a deer's range because that deer might show up anywhere. In the cold weather of the late season, that deer will be easier to pinpoint. He'll be in that good cover near his favored food source. And no amount of hunting effort in the open woods or the heavy cover, where the deer aren't spending any time, is going to be productive.

Several years ago, I spent two full days still-hunting in what I considered to be excellent cover late in the season after a ten-inch snowfall. I had seen deer in these areas during the first week of the season, and it just made good sense to me that the deer would still be where I had found them earlier. Yet in those two days of painstaking effort, I never cut a fresh track. The deer had simply migrated into their winter safe-havens and were moving very little.

Once I realized this, I knew that I needed to find where the deer were holed up. And after I had found those few places where the deer were meeting the different requirements of the late season, I found deer, too. It took three days of hard scouting efforts, but on the fourth day, I still-hunted into a tight cedar swamp and downed a nice 6-pointer.

It should also be noted that for some hunters, the best method for getting their late-season deer is to use snow cover to their best advantage. Because snow allows easy tracking, some energetic hunters are very successful when they cut a good buck track and then follow it. They do need to know their terrain very well, or need to have excellent compass and map reading skills, and they must be in excellent shape. They also should have a good emergency kit with them, and must be prepared to spend the night out in the woods if they get too far from their camp or car. But eventually, the trail will lead to the buck that's been making it. In fact, any hunter who is out during the late season, when temperatures and the elements can be treacherous, must have his wits about him. He should always pack at least one day's supply of a good high energy food. The clothing that he puts on in the morning needs to be well thought out. If he's going to stand for two or three hours, he'll need to layer up to keep warm. If he then plans to still-hunt through the midday, he'll need to shed some layers and carry them in a pack. When he goes back on stand in the evening, he'll need the warmth of his layers again, and he'll need to be sure that his midday efforts haven't made his underclothes damp.

His gun, muzzleloader, or bow needs to be ready for the tough, cold weather, too. Mechanisms need to be clean and functional. Regular gun oil can gel in cold weather, so a lighter grade is necessary. Bow cams need to work quietly and efficiently. And scopes must not fog up. Above all, however, a hunter needs to know his own personal mechanism.

He needs to know just how much effort he can safely exert. He needs to know that a rising wind can make 20-degree temperatures as dangerous as 20-below temperatures in a matter of minutes. And he needs to exercise plenty of good sense. With all of these cautions flagged, however, it is important to understand there is no better time to find and down a good buck than during the deep freeze of the late season. With the deer sticking to small pockets of cover, they will be easier to pinpoint. With most other hunters out of the woods, the deer will be less likely to be disturbed. And with his methods and woods skills honed and ready, a hunter may well find that his best chance for a bragging-sized buck is in the late season's deep freeze.

5

Tabletop Scouting

By Tim Rutledge
(July 2000)

Knowing where to set up on opening morning requires an investment of time and practice. I get a head start by scouting before I even leave home.

When I'm looking to hunt an unfamiliar section of property, I get a good set of maps of the area. The most important map is the topographical quad. Topo quads are available from your local map stores, or they can be ordered directly from the United States Geological Service (www.usgs.gov). There are several types and scales available, but the one most suited to table-top scouting is the 7.5-minute quadrangle. One sheet generally costs about $5. Typically, at least some part of the property is on the next sheet, so I wind up getting several sheets to cover the entire property. Topo maps are available in digital format from the USGS and other vendors, and some allow you to select portions of map sheets to print.

Other helpful maps include aerial photographs, plat books, and road maps, just to mention a few. Many hunting camps have developed sketches showing the roads, food plots, houses, stands, and boundaries. The quality of these maps ranges from basic to complex, but all are useful in scouting.

Once you have collected the maps, spread out your data and get ready to put the pieces together. The best way to find locations with the highest potential, before you ever set foot on the land, is to ask one question: What will be influencing deer where and when I am hunting them?

Hunting pressure, food sources, cover, roads, access, natural topography, and historical travel corridors all dictate where deer will go during the hunting season. Our goal in scouting, whether from the field or at the kitchen table, is to determine which of these influences will act upon deer during the season.

The first things I look for when scouting from the tabletop are the man-made borders. Certain boundaries will, by default, limit where we can hunt and how we get there. How the neighbors use their property is also an important factor. A game preserve next door makes for a different hunting situation than would a farm, plant, or another hunting camp. Do your

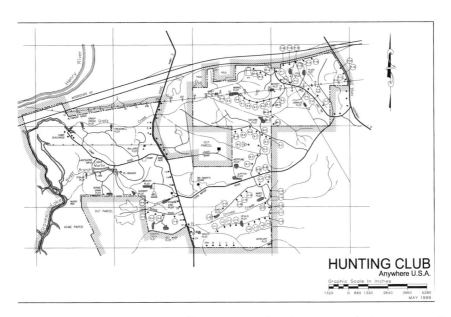

Homemade camp maps are effective in guiding hunters to their setups and keeping them aware of access routes. *Credit: Tim Rutledge*

neighbors hunt? Are there food sources, clear-cuts, swamps, or agricultural fields next door?

Once I know my limits, I check out the land. Aerial photographs are extremely useful if they are reasonably current. However, even a photo several years old can be helpful in showing where things are and the relative age of the timber. You can see the limits of a clear-cut or se-lect cut operations by an aerial photo. Even if the photo is a few years old, you can tell if the trees of one section are larger than those of the next. Access roads put in for timber operations become very handy when trying to get a large deer out of the woods—if you know where they are. I once used an old aerial photo of an area to see the features right after it was clear-cut. The trees were grown up in the field when I hunted the land, but the old photo showed the roads and other features better than x-ray vision could.

Other notable man-made items are roads, buildings, food plots, fields, bridges, accesses, camps, and gates. Study the area and get a feel for where everything is located. This is not only important for successful hunt-ing, but for safety, too, as was driven home to me several years ago.

I was hunting from a ground blind about halfway up the slope of a ridge, behind a food plot. A large racked buck was running along the top of the ridge above me. I turned to fire, but stopped when I remembered that there was a farmhouse almost directly in line with the shot. Since I knew from the map where the farmhouse was, even though it was on the neighbor's prop-erty, I passed on a potentially dangerous shot. Oh well; I know where he lives.

Use of the land is also an important factor in tabletop scouting. While most of us hunt in or near woods, we often find that the edges of the different types of terrain make for great hunting. Deer use thin areas as travel lanes and feed on the newer greenery that grows on edges. Topo maps are shaded green for the areas with woods cover, and aren't shaded for the open areas. But find out when the map was made. There should be a date under the name of the topo sheet that tells you when the map was made, plus another date, generally in purple, that gives the date of any re-visions. My experience is that you cannot rely only on the green of the map; you need to check it by other sources as well. This is where other maps, especially aerial photos, come into play.

Agricultural fields can be a prime factor during hunting season. At certain times of year, crops pull deer like a magnet. Fields can often be found on the map while you are at the kitchen table. Check out the actual location prior to hunting to see what crop is in the field, its age, and how animals are using it.

The road network on a piece of land is a very important part of tabletop scouting. While I have earned my reputation as a "hoofer" around the hunting camp, I still want to know the closest point to which I can get an ATV or vehicle to retrieve a harvested animal. I have worn off spots of hair while dragging deer, but I certainly don't recommend it. Most of the time, I park as far away from my stand as I can get, and then walk there. However, after the shot, I can drive right to the animal.

I made a poor shot on a doe a few years back, from the same ridgeline I mentioned earlier. The shot forced me to trail her for nearly 800 yards. Well, that half-mile put me deep in a thick pine plantation, a long way from my truck. Since I knew, from the map, of an old logging road at the top of the next ridge, I dragged my deer up to the road to where my truck could reach it. From there, I left my deer, rifle, pack, and most of my clothes, and walked the almost two miles to my truck. And after my trailing, dragging, and walking, I still had to clean the deer. All hunters should have such an adventure to motivate them to improve their marksmanship! The point is that, because I knew where the old road was, I minimized the amount of work needed to recover the animal.

Man-made features can attract or repel deer. Look at the feature, what time of year you will be hunting, and decide how the feature will influence deer behavior. Corn, soybeans, wheat, or other crops in season will almost surely pull deer from great distances. In hard years, you might even find deer searching the old fields after harvest. A fresh clearcut generally repels deer, except for early or late in the day or during the rut. The same clear-cut after six months will be a smorgasbord of new growth that attracts deer. After several years, this same clear-cut will provide enough cover to allow deer to feel comfortable crossing it in broad daylight.

After taking stock of the man-made influences upon the deer and the land, consider the natural characteristics that can influence deer behavior. The first and easiest items to look for are rivers, ridges, ravines, saddles, and other topographical features that funnel or direct the movement of deer. While I have seen deer swim the deepest rivers and climb the steepest slopes, they usually follow the most direct travel routes.

I recently joined a hunting camp and was faced with the very task of scouting I am describing here. As I began to review the information at hand, I immediately noticed a drainage that came from the pine plantations out to the flats near a creek. With the lay of the land on both sides of the creek and the saddles across the tops of the hills, I knew this area held great promise. During our first work day at camp, we "took a break" to look at the drainage. Sure enough, we were rewarded with a network of trails that had a good mix of old and new sign. The task from which we were taking our break had been to clear a road above this drainage. Now we could see along this road several places where the deer had been crossing to get down to and up from the bottom. In fact, we saw two deer—one with a handsome, velvety rack—heading down to the creek.

Pay close attention to the traditional trails that deer use. I have watched deer use the same trails year after year, even after major shifts in land cover or use. This proves especially useful during the rut, since bucks are following does that might have used the trail at night. You can take advantage of these runs when you are looking at a new area on land you've already hunted. I have taken my maps and extended the trails I know about to see where they go. This has led me to creek crossings, bottlenecks, and other parts of the same trail network.

A favorite technique of mine is to look in swamps for "islands"— small pieces of land that are a few feet above the rest of the swamp. Many times these areas don't flood, or not as often as the rest, and are covered by hardwoods, which produce acorn (and other mast) crops. The hard part is figuring out how to get to them without making too much noise. But that's for another article. Watch these areas when the swamps flood.

Most states have laws about hunting game on islands of a certain number of acres. This means you might not be able to hunt islands unless you have a land bridge to them. Generally, they are elevated sanctuaries for animals, which provide an excellent defense system and an abundant source of food, even in the driest years. Not all islands are visible from the maps, but they're out there, and deer like them.

A footnote to the island topic is a ridge in the swamp. Swampy areas along river courses, which tend to flood, sometimes develop a ridge along the edges of the main river or stream channel. These act as levees and are a few feet higher than the neighboring swamp. Sometimes palmettos or similar plants grow along the edges of the rivers. This tells you the land is a bit higher than everything else is.

Keep an eye out for openings at the forest edge. Look closely, and you'll see that a doe has just entered the field from an opening in the left-center of the photo. This area would merit further investigation. *Credit: Tim Rutledge*

Knowing what crops lie where is crucial in creating your hunting setup. In this photo, the wheat field on the left, when harvested, will host deer munching on the residuals. On the right, the corn field will attract deer while it grows. *Credit: Tim Rutledge*

Topographical maps are excellent resources for recognizing property boundaries. However, hunters should be sure the borders shown are current.

Credit: Tim Rutledge

Another way to find these ridges is to look at the foliage from a hill, bridge, or aerial photo. Trees like water, white, live, or pin oaks that tend to grow on the ridges have different types and colors of leaves, and lose them at different times than the gums or cypress within the swamps.

There is no trick to tabletop scouting. Simply scout an area at home to reduce the amount of time you must spend in the field, looking for the right hunting locations. There are no guarantees that the spot you find from the tabletop will be the perfect setup. However, by taking time to become familiar with the land before you go afield, you'll cover more ground and do it more effectively.

6

Tracking Wounded Deer

BUCKMASTERS

By Joel S. Fawcett
(September 1997)

Slowly, a step at a time, I still-hunted my way along an old tote road that dated back to the days of river drives, crosscut saws, and horse-drawn logging equipment. The ancient horse trail cut back into the woods from the shore of the St. Croix River near my home in the village of Grand Lake Stream, Maine, a few miles south of the Canadian border, and meandered its way through several miles of mixed hemlock, fir, and spruce thickets. Fresh sign was everywhere, and I hunted with a great deal of anticipation.

A couple of hours into the morning's hunt, I came upon a table-size scrape beneath a small fir tree, and a licking branch had been nipped off and deposited in the pawing. "Ah-ha, a dominant buck's breeding scrape," I muttered to myself. I searched the surrounding cover meticulously from both a standing and a squatting position, and while thus engaged I noticed a big spruce tree with some odd looking branches down low. A closer look revealed I was eyeballing the antlers of a big buck. However, outside of his heavy-

The author examines blood on a leaf. Mark that spot, then search for the next spot or splotch of blood. *Credit: Lillian Fawcett*

beamed antlers, the critter was hidden from sight. I inched forward about half a step, and from there I could see about a four-inch patch of hide behind the buck's shoulder. If I attempted to move ahead further to obtain a better sight picture, he'd likely spook, and in the heavy cover I'd probably never get a shot. Slowly, I shouldered my 7mm-08 rifle, released the safety, carefully lined up my crosshairs on the patch of hide, and squeezed the trigger.

However, at the sound of the shot, the big hombre switched ends and rapidly bounded out of view. I couldn't believe it. The sight picture was perfect, the shot felt good, yet the animal didn't appear to be the least bit distressed when he bounded away into the willywags. I was dismayed until I hiked over to the area where the deer had been standing, and here a careful search revealed a small clump of gray hair. My hopes rose.

I followed the buck's wake for perhaps fifty yards and found nothing, and I was about to conclude my bullet had only grazed the animal. Then, I noticed something glistening among the pine needles. It was blood! A little farther on, I found more BB-size spots of blood. Then, the splotches got larger, and the blood trail became easy to follow. Suddenly, the blood sign vanished completely. I marked the spot, began circling, and in a small gully some forty feet from the last blood splotches, I found the 10-point, 237-pound buck piled up. My bullet had punctured the buck's lung, yet he had traveled well over 100 yards through heavy cover before collapsing.

Every responsible hunter wants to secure a quick, clean, one-shot harvest, but it doesn't always happen this way. No matter how conscientiously you hunt and shoot, sooner or later a deer will unexpectedly move just as you squeeze off a shot, an unseen twig or sapling will deflect your bullet, or some other unforeseen circumstance will occur, and instead of tumbling to the ground as expected, a deer will bound away into the cover.

When this occurs, pay close attention to the animal's reactions as it heads for the thickets. Most deer will spook at the sound of the shot, but if the critter flinches, droops its tail, humps its back, sags, stumbles, or exhibits any other abnormal response—it has taken lead. Occasionally, as in the above situation, a mortally injured deer will give no indication it has been hurt, but will bound away as if unscathed. Unless it's been hit in the brain, spinal cord, or neck vertebrae, there's no guarantee a fatally wounded deer will drop in its tracks. An animal hit in the lungs, heart, liver, or jugular is dead on its feet, but it may still run 100 yards or more before piling up.

Other considerations may also come into play, but more than anything else, poor marksmanship is why hunters wound game. Some nimrods I've known never fire a shot through their deer musket from one season to the next, and when they miss or wound a deer on an easy shot, they place the blame on their gun, scope, the shell caliber they're using, or on something else. Rarely do they fault their own poor shooting.

It's beyond my comprehension how anyone can enter the deer woods with a rifle they haven't fired in a year or more; or worse yet, with a new gun or scope that's only been bore-sighted at the factory or by a gunsmith. I was a registered Maine guide for 18 years, and several of my first-time clients followed this modus operandi until I refused to guide them unless they first accompanied me to a nearby gravel pit and sighted in. Some of them couldn't even hit the paper at 25 yards, yet they were set to enter the woods and hunt deer. The only way to become a competent marksman is to expend a lot of ammunition. Prior to opening day each season, I like to push at least 50 to 100 rounds or more through my deer gun, and I also visit a firing range frequently in the off-season. Such a policy gives me confidence in my shooting, and when I pull the trigger, I don't need a reaction from the deer to tell me I've scored a clean harvest.

Just because a deer you shoot at in heavy cover doesn't fall until it's out of sight should not be taken as an indication that the animal has not been hit. However, some irresponsible and inexperienced hunters misinterpret the critter's apparently healthy retreat as a sign that they missed, and thus a perfectly hit deer may end up as bear, coyote, and raven fodder. The responsible hunter makes it a rule to thoroughly check out every shot for evidence of a hit before assuming the animal is unhurt.

Once you've taken a shot and the deer doesn't drop in its tracks, then pick out a landmark near where the deer was standing, and hot-foot it right over there. Otherwise it's very easy to confuse the spot with its look-alike surroundings. When you arrive on the scene, if you find no indications of a hit, mark the spot with your hat, bandanna, handkerchief, or other colorful object, and fan out in ever-widening circles searching for hair, blood, bone splinters, broken branches, scuff marks in the forest duff, or any other clues indicating a deer in trouble.

There is a great deal of controversy, even among veteran deer hunters and guides, about what to do if the deer takes off wounded. Some claim it's best to wait for at least half an hour before taking up the trail to allow the deer to lie down and stiffen up. However, I like to get on the trail of a wounded whitetail immediately. When a big-game caliber bullet strikes a deer, it causes shock. Give the critter an opportunity to lie down and rest, and it may recover from the initial shock, particularly if it's hit in a non-vital area. If this occurs, it becomes much more difficult—sometimes impossible—to track your quarry down.

A deer shot in the paunch, hams, shoulder, or leg, for example, does not leak large amounts of blood, unless an artery is cut. If allowed to lie down, the animal's tallow will sometimes plug the bullet hole; to trail a wounded deer leaving no blood spoor on hard ground is an almost impossible task, even for an expert tracker.

On the other hand, a closely pursued whitetail will not get a chance to rest and the wound will remain open and bleeding. Also, while waiting, the blood sign may dry, turn brown, and become difficult to detect; tracks will lose their freshness; and other sign such as bent-over grass, scuffed leaves, and so on, will become less conspicuous, thus making a difficult tracking job out of what perhaps would have been an easy one. Additionally, in most regions the hunter who records the anchoring shot usually puts his tags on the deer; therefore, in heavily hunted areas, nimrods who don't get right on the trail of a wounded deer can very easily lose their game to another hunter.

However, this doesn't mean one should go crashing after a wounded deer, carelessly popping brush, rustling leaves, and cracking shell ice or sloshing water. This would likely cause panic and lead to a long tracking job. Instead, follow the deer's wake just as quietly and furtively as you would if stalking a healthy whitetail.

One of the first things I look for when I get on the back trail of a wounded deer is a clue to how seriously the animal is injured. Bright red blood usually indicates a hit in a vital area—the heart or an artery—or if the blood is frothy, I know I've connected on a lung shot. However, not all lung- and heart-shot deer leak blood. Some bleed internally until they collapse. If you discover any of these signs, you should find your deer piled up within 150 yards or less.

The discovery of dark red blood is not so encouraging. This usually indicates a shot in the paunch, shoulder, hams, leg, or other non-vital tissue, and frequently indicates a long trailing job. A whitetail hit in the hams or back leg will show blood around a rear track, while a deer wounded in the shoulder or front leg will leave blood around a front hoof print, and a gut-shot deer will often show flecks of partly digested forage in the blood. A whitetail hit in the hams or paunch will not travel fast, will lie down frequently, and won't push out easily when jumped. It may take a while, but these animals should be recovered.

A deer shot in the leg will usually leave only three tracks and the drag mark of the broken leg, and it'll drip blood on the trail. You should be able to collect a deer with a broken hind leg, since if hotly pursued and forced to travel, he'll soon become fatigued, but the chances of recovering a deer shot in the front leg are slim. He'll flee with just about as much stamina and be just as difficult to track down as a healthy animal.

While following a blood trail, don't become so wrapped up in searching for sign that you neglect to inspect the trail up ahead. Every few steps, I pause and examine the cover with both my naked eye and my binoculars for sight of my quarry. It's not necessary to search very far from the trail.

A wounded deer may lie down or lean against a tree to regain its strength, but practically always this will be on or just off the trail. He's not going to fool around with backtracking, circling, or any of the other tricky maneuvers healthy deer often use to confuse their pursuers.

If the trail becomes faint, I get down on my hands and knees and carefully examine the forest floor for blood, scuff marks in the leaves, tracks, freshly broken twigs, and bent-over grass or bushes, and I also inspect the branches and trunks of nearby trees and bushes for blood. Sometimes it will only be a pinhead drop of blood that tells me I'm on the right course. If the blood sign peters out or is questionable, backtrack to the last confirmed sign and conduct a careful search of the area for additional clues. Often the blood trail will start up again further on.

However, if you should lose the trail completely, all is not lost. The escape route of a wounded whitetail is predictable. Invariably, a solidly hit animal will make a beeline for heavy cover, and more often than not this will be handy to a stream, swamp, bog, or pond where the animal can wallow in the water and mud and soothe its wounds. If there was considerable bleeding, the deer will also crave water to replace the lost body fluids. Therefore, use the deer's known direction of travel, a topo map of the area, and a compass to direct you to the nearest dense cover and adjacent water hole. Chances are the buck you're trailing will not be far away.

Incidentally, in familiar woods you can sometimes take advantage of a wounded whitetail's typical straight line retreat to dense woods and water by making a quick circle and intercepting your quarry before it reaches its chosen sanctuary. However, in an unfamiliar bailiwick, it's best to stick to the deer's spoor rather than attempting any shortcuts, perhaps becoming confused and losing the blood trail permanently.

In snow-covered terrain, your tracking problems are solved—or are they? A few years ago, a client I was guiding took a hurried shot at a 6-pointer we jumped. The deer stumbled, but he recovered quickly, and bounded into a nearby stand of popple (aspen) trees. Tracking was easy. Several inches of new snow blanketed the forest, and the buck also left a fair blood sign. We followed the critter to a spruce, fir, and hemlock knoll, and here several other sets of similar size tracks joined the ones we were following. Then, our quarry stopped bleeding, and a short distance further, the trail divided into three divergent trails, and deer tracks led down each path. For a while I wasn't sure which way we should go, but then on one path I noticed a couple of tracks splayed off to one side, and a short distance beyond, the critter had bumped into a fir tree. Well, healthy animals don't often do that. We followed, and about a quarter of a mile further on, we stumbled onto the paunch-shot deer, and my hunter made a clean, fatal shot.

When tracking a wounded whitetail, keep your ears tuned not only for cracking branches, scuffling in the leaves, labored breathing, or other indications of a deer experiencing problems, but also for the alarm signals of other residents of the forest. A red squirrel will sometimes chatter at an injured deer, but no creature on earth takes greater delight in noisily announcing the whereabouts of a wounded animal than a blue jay does. If, while following the wake of a deer you've hit, you hear a blue jay going absolutely bananas, make a beeline for the sound. I'll almost guarantee he's screeching at your quarry.

Also, keep your eyes peeled for ravens or whisky jacks (Canada jays) heading for the same spot. These scavengers seem to possess an uncanny intuition of when and where an animal is about to expire, and gather to feast on the remains.

Every person who enters the deer woods with gun or bow assumes a moral responsibility to make a conscientious effort to recover any deer he or she hits. Recovering a solidly hit deer is not difficult. All it takes is the ability to read and interpret sign, a knowledge of how a whitetail is likely to react when he takes lead, and the patience and determination to track a wounded animal down. If these skills are not in your repertoire, they can easily be acquired by observing behavioral tendencies, and practicing your tracking techniques on healthy whitetails in the off-season.

7

Small Details for Big Farmland Bucks

By Jim Hole, Jr.
(Hunting Annual—1994)

Bowhunting for trophy whitetails is considered the ultimate challenge by many hunters. Surprisingly enough, however, taking a trophy whitetail can be a relatively easy task if a hunter pays absolute attention to detail and proceeds with a predetermined plan.

There are many obstacles which stand between success and failure of the trophy whitetail bowhunter, none of which can't be overcome if the hunter follows practical guidelines. The following tips and techniques are of extreme importance in getting a hunter an opportunity at a trophy whitetail. Here are my six pet tips and their applications.

Take your time while scouting—even in the pre-season. Go quickly, and you'll probably miss crucial clues. *Credit: Eric Crosan*

Scouting

One of the most important components that the whitetail hunter faces is scouting. If the hunter is capable of locating a good whitetail and analyzing its pattern without disturbing the natural travel routes, he is well on his way to taking his trophy. The problem which many hunters face is their failure to set up and watch a particular buck from a distance. It seems that the average hunter doesn't exercise the patience needed to scout out of bow range. Although many hunters feel their time is best spent in a stand where they may get a shot at the deer they are hunting, the chance of success greatly increases when the deer's travel routes are analyzed at a distance and then hunted at a later time.

In order for the hunter to watch from a distance, a tree stand and binoculars are required. In areas where deer have experienced some hunting pressure, the transition from bedding to feeding areas usually occurs during the evening in dim light. This is when the hunter requires high quality binoculars with good light gathering ability.

Generally, binoculars should have an exit pupil of at least 5mm, which is the maximum pupil size of the human eye. For example, a pair of 7X50 binoculars has an exit pupil of 7.15 mm, which is calculated by dividing 50 by 7. Compact binoculars have a limited low-light ability. For example, 7X26 binoculars have an exit pupil of 3.72 mm, which results in a reduction of the low-light visual ability of the hunter.

A binocular which has been used extensively on Alberta hunts is the Swarovski 8X30, which is very bright in low light and very convenient due to its compact design.

To illustrate the point of scouting from a distance, I recall one hunt from the fall of 1989. At dusk, a non-typical appeared 75 yards from where he was expected. The buck traveled out into the alfalfa field and began to feed for the night. Leaving the area as quietly as I had approached it, I was certain the buck never knew he had been watched.

Once the pattern has been analyzed, it then becomes easy for the hunter to select an appropriate stand site and wait for the proper conditions to hunt the particular buck for the first, and hopefully only, time. My long distance spotting proved just the ticket for my hunter, John Trout, Jr., who later bagged that very buck.

Preserving a Site

Once the hunter has done his homework and has found what he feels is a productive site, it then becomes very important to preserve the site until productive hunting conditions prevail. In the case of John Trout's hunt, the buck was left until conditions were exactly right, and success came on the first attempt. John rattled in the 15-point, 260-pound white-tail, and took him at eighteen yards.

One of the most common mistakes made by hunters is hunting a would-be productive site prior to having ideal conditions, and subsequently spooking the deer. Alarming the deer educates the animals, and in most cases puts the hunter back where he began, having to locate another productive site. Mature whitetails are the most sensitive to any disturbance. Smaller bucks and does may be alarmed in some instances, and within 24 hours, return to their normal travel patterns. The trophies, however, very rarely return quickly to their normal patterns after being alarmed. Some Alberta whitetails I've observed were spooked in September and did not return to their normal travel routes until late November or December.

One technique which has been very useful on trophy hunts has been to have several different stands in place, offering the hunter several options. For example, one stand may be ideal for a northwest wind, while another stand may be best in a southeast wind. This will accommodate the hunter for either wind direction. Under no circumstances should a hunter enter a stand unless the wind is favorable for that specific stand.

Wind Analysis

Most hunters agree that the whitetail's most difficult sense to escape is his sense of smell. If a buck sees or hears something, in many cases he will remain still to further investigate; but if a hunter's scent is carried to the nose of a whitetail, it will most always leave the area with little hesitation.

A successful bowhunter must be efficient in analyzing wind direction in order to play the game in his favor, rather than the deer's. Most hunters are well aware of staying downwind of game, but at times this can be a difficult task. One such time is Alberta's early bow season, which runs during the months of September and October. Typically during the season,

51

temperatures vary from 10 degrees to 75 degrees Fahrenheit. During cooler weather, winds are usually consistent and easy to work with, but in warm temperatures, inconsistent winds can present the hunter with quite a challenge.

A typical scenario is an alfalfa field in which a hunter has located a good buck. During the warm evening hunt, the wind is light but consistent until the sun settles below the horizon. At this point, the change in air temperature almost always causes wind direction to reverse. What seemed to be an ideal setup has now turned into the hunter's worst nightmare. If he's smart, he will observe from a distance. Attempting to hunt the buck under those circumstances will probably spook the buck and spoil the location. This is an example of how a good site can be ruined by hunting in marginal conditions such as warm weather.

There are two solutions to this problem. The first is to not hunt the site until cooler weather prevails; or, to hunt during the warm weather but wait until just before sunset to get on the stand. If the hunter must wait until sunset to get into position, he will have little time to hunt, and he must be able to get to his stand quickly. Also, due to the hunter's late arrival, deer may be spooked by his approach. Luckily, there is a solution to getting a hunter to his stand quickly in farmland country.

Using a Vehicle

Fortunately in farmland areas, all of the deer, including mature bucks, are very familiar with farm vehicles and motorized travel. Almost all hunters have witnessed how alarmed a deer becomes by a human walking nearby, as opposed to a vehicle traveling in the same area.

Incorporating a vehicle into some hunting situations can be a very effective tool if done properly. There is no doubt that the most effective way to set up on a mature whitetail is with no disturbance whatsoever; but in the event of a hunter trying to get into position late, a vehicle can be a great asset.

An example which illustrates the value of using a vehicle occurred on September 13, 1989. Fellow Alberta bowhunter Ken Elder and I were hunting Edmonton's Bow-Only zone. The temperature was in the mid 70s; very hot by Alberta standards. We arrived at the alfalfa field 2½ hours before dark. Two stands were placed in predetermined locations and left until just before sunset. As the sun dropped below the horizon, the air cooled and the wind reversed, which allowed both stands to be quickly occupied thanks to a quick drive to the stand sites in a vehicle. Now with favorable conditions prevailing, both hunters were in place. Within 20 minutes, four bucks appeared and fed within 18 yards of my stand. A well placed arrow took the best of the four bucks: a non-typical, 16-point, 260-pounder!

There is no doubt that in this particular case, an early hunter would have been easily detected. The wind had done a complete 180-degree switch, which would have scented the bedding area. Although the vehicle can be an effective tool as discussed in this case, there are times when a hunter has consistent winds, and an approach on foot can be the best method.

Approaching a Stand

Hunters must understand the general travel routes of the deer they intend to hunt in order to get to a tree stand with no disturbance. Not only must the hunter keep his stand site advantageous with respect to wind direction, he must also keep his route of travel from carrying any scent to the deer he is about to set up on.

As the hunter travels toward his stand on foot, a scent trail is laid down step after step. It is very important to use footwear with a rubber bottom, especially for stand hunting. The rubber bottom helps to minimize the transfer of odors from the foot to the ground. Also, this pair of boots should only be used for hunting in order to keep all foreign odors to a minimum.

Walking to the tree stand requires a certain amount of work. Dress for travel should always be light to minimize perspiration. Also, a small backpack should be used to carry warm clothes and gear for ease of travel. It does a hunter no good to wear clean clothes if he sweats them up during travel and transmits a strong odor once on the stand.

One of the most important aspects of stand hunting is when to travel to and from the tree stand. Most hunters have learned to travel to a stand during the animal's bedding time for the evening hunt, but very few hunters exercise the patience to wait and leave a stand once the deer have cleared the immediate area after dark. If departure from the stand takes place when deer are in hearing distance, it takes little time for the bucks to pattern the hunters and stay clear of the stand. Good low light binoculars are essential for the hunter to check the immediate area and to make an undetected departure. Mature bucks seem to have a great talent for locating tree stands and staying well out of bow range. For this reason, it is imperative that a hunter makes the utmost effort to keep his stand a secret.

Stand Sites and Installation

Placing a tree stand for a bowhunter that does not affect the travel patterns of deer frequenting the area is a challenge. The hunter has two options at his disposal. First, the stand can be placed just prior to its use so a buck has no opportunity to find the stand; or, a stand can be placed and left until the deer becomes used to its presence.

However you intend to set up your stand, there are a few things which can help to minimize disturbance. First, use a small pack to carry your tree-stand tools. Your tools should include rubber gloves, limb shears, and a limb saw.

The rubber gloves are used to install steps and clear limbs without leaving scent. It would be pointless to install a scentless stand and steps and cover them with human odor in the process. The limb shears are used to trim only the necessary branches. The limb saw is used to clear large branches that can't be cleared with the smaller shears. The limb saw leaves more scent behind as it produces sawdust. Shears make a clean cut and create less odor from the tree. Be sure to leave no foreign odors at your stand, such as garbage or urine.

If a vehicle is used to take you to your stand site, odor can be drastically reduced by working right from the vehicle, never touching the ground during installation. It is important to place the stand making as few changes to the area as possible.

The consistently successful trophy whitetail bowhunter must pay grave attention to detail. There have been countless stories told of how close a hunter has been to capitalizing on his opportunity, when the smallest detail quickly ended what seemed to be an almost surefire thing. The dedicated whitetail enthusiast must continually strive to put all he can in his favor to minimize the problems that can arise when closing in on his chance of a lifetime. When it comes to whitetails, it's the details that cost you.

Bucks for the Record

The BTR Golden Laurel Citation

The BTR's (Buckmasters Trophy Records) prestigious Golden Laurel Citation (GLC) is awarded annually for the most significant trophy whitetail record entry for the year's scoring period. The recipients receive the GLC at the Buckmasters Expo, held in August of each year in Montgomery, Alabama. While fortunate hunters who harvest these great bucks receive the GLC, the award is given to honor North America's most spectacular and magnificent whitetail bucks.

The following pages highlight some of those magnificent bucks, plus provide information on the scoring system. A sample score sheet is also included, should you get a book buck yourself.

Fulton Buck
1996 Golden Laurel Citation Winner
Score: 321 7/8
Hunter: Tony Fulton
Date of Harvest: January 5, 1995
Locale of Harvest: Winston County, Mississippi
Weapon Category: Centerfire Rifle
Antler Classification: Irregular

Collora Buck
1997 Golden Laurel Citation Winner
Score: 204 6/8
Hunter: Sam Collora
Date of Harvest: October 11, 1996
Locale: Henry County, Iowa
Weapon Category: Compound Bow
Antler Classification: Typical

Remmers Buck
1998 Golden Laurel Citation Winner
Score 253 5/8
Hunter: Jamie Remmers
Date of Harvest: December 7, 1997
Locale: Marion County, Kansas
Weapon Category: Centerfire Rifle
Antler Classification: Irregular

Beeman Buck
1999 Golden Laurel Citation Co-Winner
Score: 259 5/8
Hunter: Bobby Beeman
Date of Harvest: September 2, 1998
Locale: Park County, Wyoming
Weapon Category: Crossbow
Antler Classification: Irregular

Larson Buck
1999 Golden Laurel Citation Co-Winner
Score: 264 5/8˙
Hunter: Dale Larson
Date of Harvest: November 7, 1998
Locale: Pottawatomie County, Kansas
Weapon Category: Compound Bow
Antler Classification: Irregular

Stovall Buck
2000 Golden Laurel Citation Winner
Score: 203 6/8
Hunter: James Stovall
Date of Harvest: September 25, 1999
Locale: Pasco County, Florida
Weapon Category: Compound Bow
Antler Classification: Irregular (Velvet)

Beatty Buck
2001 Golden Laurel Citation Winner
Score: 286 4/8
Hunter: Mike Beatty
Date of Harvest: November 8, 2000
Locale: Greene County, Ohio
Weapon Category: Compound Bow
Antler Classification: Irregular

Zaft Buck
2002 Golden Laurel Citation Co-Winner
Score: 205 7/8
Hunter: Wayne Zaft
Date of Harvest: October 8, 2001
Locale: Parkland, Alberta, Canada
Weapon Category: Compound Bow
Antler Classification: Typical

Wilson Buck
2002 Golden Laurel Citation Co-Winner
Score: 303 4/8
Hunter: Troy Wilson
Date of Harvest: October 27, 2001
Locale: Gallatin County, Kentucky
Weapon Category: Blackpowder
Antler Classification: Irregular (Velvet)

In BTR scoring the inside spread measurement is considered supplemental data. It is not added into the rack's official score because it is a measurement of air—not antler.

Mike Beatty with the Golden Laurel Citation, presented to him by BTR
Executive Director Russell Thornberry.

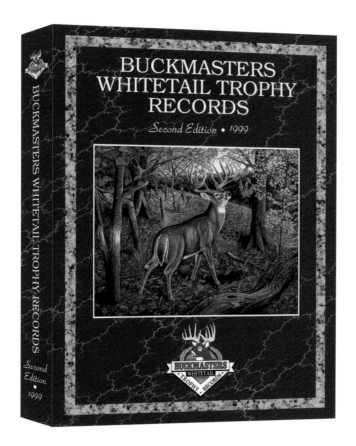

Buckmasters Whitetail Trophy Records

"Buckmasters Whitetail Trophy Records" is published in a handsome hardbound book every three years, with the third and newest edition available in Sept. 2002. "Buckmasters Whitetail Trophy Records" is the only comprehensive whitetail record-keeping agency offering categorical coverage of all hunting weapons including centerfire rifles, shotguns, blackpowder rifles, handguns, compound bows, crossbows, recurve bows, and longbows, with four antler classifications: Perfect, Typical, Semi-Irregular and Irregular, and in every weapon category. The BTR's 3rd Edition contains more than 7,000 trophy whitetail entries in all weapons categories, including pick-ups and shed antlers.

Buckmasters "Full-Credit Scoring System"

No Penalties!

No Deductions!

What you see is what you get!

The major difference between other scoring systems and the one behind "Buckmasters Whitetail Trophy Records" is that the BTR has eliminated the concept of deductions, which often keep prize antlers out of record books.

Buckmasters, the nation's largest deer hunting association with more than 370,000 members, developed the "Full-Credit Scoring System" and corresponding record book.

The philosophy of Buckmasters' Full-Credit Scoring System is to measure and record white-tailed deer antlers without forcing them to conform to a criterion of perfect symmetry. The Full-Credit Scoring System takes nothing away from the rack. It simply measures every inch of antler and classifies each rack into one of four antler classifications.

The Buckmasters system can be distinguished from other whitetail scoring methods in these nine important areas:

1. The Buckmasters system does not deduct the differences between lengths of opposing typical points.

2. It does not include the inside spread measurement in the official score because it is a measurement of air, not antler.

3. Since the inside spread between the main beams is not added into the rack's official score, a rack with a broken skull plate can still be entered into the BTR record book.

4. There are four classifications of antlers: Perfect, Typical, Semi-Irregular and Irregular.

5. Minimum score is the same for each of the four classifications of antlers. The minimum score for all firearms-harvested deer is 140 inches. A minimum score of 105 inches is required for all bow-harvested deer. These minimum scores may sound low until you realize that the inside spread credit is not included.

6. The BTR system provides categories for all types of firearms, which include centerfire rifles, handguns, shotguns and blackpowder guns. There are separate categories for compound bows, recurves, longbows and even crossbows. The "Pick-Up" category is for racks that have been found rather than harvested by a hunter. The minimum score for this category is 140 inches. There is even a category for sheds, which are measured only as a right or a left antler, not as a pair. Minimum score for shed antlers is 75 inches.

7. No drying time is required before antlers can be measured.

8. The BTR also has a separate category for antlers in velvet.

9. In addition, there is opportunity for entry for bucks taken behind game-proof fences, providing they meet the entry criteria noted on the BTR Code of Ethics for hunting on Game-Proof Fenced Properties.

For more information about having your rack entered into "Buckmasters Whitetail Trophy Records," or for information about becoming an official Buckmasters scorer, write: BTR Administrator Aduston Rogers, P.O. Box 244022, Montgomery, AL 36124-4022; or call him at (800) 240-3337.

HARD ANTLER   **VELVET**

BUCKMASTERS
WHITETAIL
TROPHY · RECORDS

SAMPLE SCORESHEET

FREE-ROAMING_____   HIGH FENCE_____

IRREGULAR POINTS			
RIGHT ANTLER		LEFT ANTLER	
1		1	
2		2	
3		3	
4		4	
5		5	
6		6	
7		7	
8		8	
9		9	
10		10	
11		11	
12		12	
13		13	
14		14	
15		15	
16		16	
17		17	
18		18	
19		19	
20		20	
21		21	
22		22	
23		23	
24		24	
25		25	

SUPPLEMENTARY DATA

1. TOTAL NUMBER OF POINTS PER ANTLER	R.	L.
2. TIP TO TIP SPREAD		
3. GREATEST SPREAD		
4. INSIDE SPREAD BETWEEN MAIN BEAMS		
5. NUMBER OF IRREGULAR POINTS	R.	L.
6. TOTAL INCHES OF IRREGULAR POINTS (IRR)		
7. LENGTH OF MAIN BEAM (MB)		
8. LENGTH OF FIRST POINT (P1)		
9. LENGTH OF SECOND POINT (P2)		
10. LENGTH OF THIRD POINT (P3)		
11. LENGTH OF FOURTH POINT (P4)		
12. LENGTH OF FIFTH POINT (P5)		
13. LENGTH OF SIXTH POINT (P6)		
14. LENGTH OF SEVENTH POINT (P7)		
15. LENGTH OF EIGHTH POINT (P8)		
16. LENGTH OF NINTH POINT (P9)		
17. LENGTH OF TENTH POINT (P10)		
18. FIRST CIRCUMFERENCE MEASUREMENT (C1)		
19. SECOND CIRCUMFERENCE MEASUREMENT (C2)		
20. THIRD CIRCUMFERENCE MEASUREMENT (C3)		
21. FOURTH CIRCUMFERENCE MEASUREMENT (C4)		

SCORE PER SIDE

OFFICIAL SCORE

COMPOSITE SCORE
(INCLUDES INSIDE SPREAD)

HARVESTED BY _____

DATE OF HARVEST _____

LOCATION OF HARVEST (County) _____ (State) _____

GUIDED BY _____

OWNER _____

ADDRESS _____

CITY _____ STATE _____ ZIP _____

PHONE ( ) _____ DATE SCORED: _____

SCORER _____ SCORER NO. _____

COLLECTED BY:
LONG BOW_____
RECURVE_____
COMPOUND_____
CROSSBOW_____
CENTERFIRE RIFLE_____
SHOTGUN_____
PISTOL_____
BLK. POWDER_____
PICK-UPS_____
SHED ANTLERS_____

CATEGORY:
PERFECT_____
TYPICAL_____
SEMI IRREGULAR_____
IRREGULAR_____
% IRR_____

MINIMUM SCORES:
FIREARMS–140
BOW/CROSSBOW–105
PICK-UPS –140
SHED ANTLERS–75

What Does YOUR Trophy Score?

Here's a BTR scoresheet you can photocopy and unofficially measure your own buck to see if it meets the minimum score for BTR entry (140 inches for all firearms and 105 for all bow and crossbow entries). If your trophy whitetail meets the minimum score, have it officially scored and entered in "Buckmasters Whitetail Trophy Records." With each official entry, you will receive a handsome, colorful and frameable BTR award certificate, as well as a listing in the next printing of the Buckmasters record book.

◆

8

Still-Hunting

By Barry Wensel
(Hunting Annual—1994)

Still-hunting is rather a gray area for me. Personally, I'm not sure if people don't really understand what still-hunting is, or if they don't generally have the patience, and therefore don't do it right. In either respect, what most people call still-hunting is not what I consider still-hunting.

Some hunters just generally "go for a walk in the woods" and say they were still-hunting. They probably were to a degree, but there's a lot more to it than that.

By my definition, still-hunting is simply a mobile stand hunter. If you're walking more than you're standing still in any one time period, you're still-hunting, in my opinion.

I love to still-hunt. It's a state of mind. Read that sentence again. It's a state of mind. It's probably one of the best ways to become one with nature.

The author prefers to still-hunt on days with light rain or cloud cover. The woods are quiet under such conditions, and enable the stealthy still-hunter to sneak up on wary bucks such as this one. *Credit: Barry Wensel*

Most people are geared too hyper to be hunters. It's not really their fault. It's just that the rigors and hustle of everyday living have us going through our routines at a much faster pace than we psychologically should be when hunting this method.

When we leave home or hunting camp or wherever in the morning, most of us tend to be in a rush to get where we're going too quickly. We're geared too high. We go to the area in fourth gear, drop down to third when we get there, and usually hunt in second gear. Some, a very few guys, hunt in first gear. I'm not even going to give you that. I'm stating that you should still-hunt completely "shut down," then shut down again.

One of the best still-hunters I've ever met told me about his "secrets" to success. He is also of the opinion that still-hunting is a state of mind. His philosophy of success is to reverse the roles. He psychologically becomes the hunted rather than the hunter.

He goes into the general area he wants to hunt at a regular pace and then lies down on the ground and closes his eyes and listens. He says if you listen long enough, sooner or later you'll hear something. It may be a squirrel cutting, a branch breaking, or a jay scolding . . . whatever; but that listening period gears him down psychologically. Then when he hears the noise, he imagines "someone" is after him, and he has to move with the utmost of caution or else he will be caught. It's a mind game, but reversing the role from hunter to hunted works for him.

Before we get into methods of still-hunting, I think, we should take into consideration the conditions that not only dictate success or failure, but determine whether you should be hunting in this way on a particular day in the first place.

Conditions must be perfect. Still-hunting is more conducive to rifle hunting than bowhunting, although it can be done with the bow. The concept is to see the animal before he sees you, slip within range, and execute your shot. Unfortunately, this is not always the case, and the animal detects the hunter first and takes off. When bowhunting, the situation is usually over if the game is jumped. Whereas with a gun, even when the game is disturbed, the hunter still has the capability to reach out and "reduce him to possession."

There's a difference between conditions being perfect and conditions being acceptable. I prefer a cloudy/overcast day to sunshine. I hate sunshine anyway. Hunting is always better on a cloudy/dreary day. You know why hunting is always better early in the morning and late evening?

It's more like a cloudy day. If the sun is shining, it's usually too hot, game is holed up, visibility is poor due to excessive shadows, I'm always squinting, sweating, etc. I hate sunshine . . . and you can quote me on that.

Anyway, I prefer a cloudy/overcast day to still-hunt. I like it even more if there's a slow drizzle occurring. I don't mean a downpour/soaker rain, I mean a little drizzle. My favorite is when it's like a heavy mist in the air. Everything is soaked, thereby keeping my noise to a minimum; and still I have dripping in the background to help cover any mistakes I happen to make.

Same with wind conditions. Most guys say they prefer no wind so they can hear. I prefer a slow steady breeze. If the woods are wet, you aren't going to hear much anyway. A deer walking on wet leaves with pointed hoofs isn't going to give you much to listen to. I'd rather have a slight, steady breeze that I can depend upon for my movement. Having it directionally steady is the most important factor. When you have "no wind" at all, there are still some slight shifts one way and then the other, ups and downs before it becomes predominant in one specific direction. An individual who is properly still-hunting is covering way too little ground and remains motionless in one particular area for too long to put up with any mild and variable wind shifts. A mild but steady breeze is better.

Always still-hunt with the breeze in your face, quartering into the wind, or at the very least, cross wind.

Speaking of wind, it's possible to be real successful still-hunting in very windy conditions. Most of us think of slipping along wet leaves in dead calm as the ideal situation. Several times I've been hunting river bottoms that were comprised of vast areas of wild rose bushes. The deer would feed on the rose hips readily, and on an extremely windy day, you could slip right up on feeding bucks. Usually, all you would see was a rack rocking back and forth over the tops of the rose bushes. I guess they were too busy trying to separate the rose hips from the stickers, because you could get right up on them.

I've also had a lot of success still-hunting on dark, misty, wet afternoons in old grown-over apple orchards. I think the moist air carries the aroma of sweet, fermenting apples down through the timber, so that the deer can't wait for nocturnal feeding. You can run them out of a wet orchard, and half an hour later, they're back.

Obviously we can't control the still-hunting conditions, but we can control other factors that improve the conditions. Take camouflage for example. Try to make your colors match the surroundings. Dark green camo tends to stand out as a dark blob against most backgrounds. In some situations, it's possible to still-hunt in softwood terrain, but usually the thickness of cover will limit your visibility and make hardwoods or semi-open terrain more conducive to slip-hunting. Color-wise, I've always preferred various shades of gray and brown over darker shades of green and black.

Other than winding you, the way most deer will catch you will be through your movement. This dictates total camouflage. When I refer to total camouflage, I'm not referring to specific camo patterns. Any dull or drab broken pattern whose color scheme blends into the surroundings works well. This also includes snow camouflage. When snow is on the ground, I'm a firm believer that a basic white camo broken up with a few dark streaks here and there will be a much better color scheme than any of the darker, regular camo patterns. Deer aren't used to seeing anything white chasing them, and don't as yet associate a white pattern with danger.

As important as any one thing, it's vital to still-hunt with a face mask and gloves. I can't stress this opinion too much. As with deer drives, you are at ground level, and therefore eye level. Other than actual mobile movement to and from your hunting area, donning a face mask whenever at ground level will increase your success dramatically. Yeah, I know it's a pain in the neck, but your chances of being seen and/or detected at eye level will be decreased greatly if you don't show them a white face floating down through the timber.

Clothing material is very important. You have to have a surface that is soft and quiet. Chamois is okay as long as it's dry. But once the fabric is wet, be it from the morning dew or precipitation, it tends to send out a mildly offensive rustle that impedes my hearing. They may not be able to detect the noise of wet chamois at any appreciable distance, but I don't like it myself. I much prefer wool, fleece, or even sweatshirt-type material. Yeah, it'll pick up burrs, but I really don't care. It's quiet.

Footwear, or lack of it, is probably another one of the most important dividing factors in successful still-hunting. After hunting barefoot with some Hawaiians, Paul Brunner gave up shoes one April and went barefoot through September. Going without any shoes for six months really toughens up your feet. They get calloused and hard, but they are superbly quiet. Unfortunately, living in the northern hemisphere and dealing with seasonal variations (snow) makes it unreasonable for us to do this. When the Hawaiians' feet crack and split, or if they get cut, they heal up, and it makes them all the more tough. When we get a cut on our bare feet, by the time it heals, the snow is flying and the season is over. You get the drift (no pun intended).

There are some happy mediums, though. I've hunted with Paul Schafer when he's worn nothing on his feet but heavy wool socks under a pair of ankle height cut-off rubbers—the kind your average white-collar businessman might wear down Wall Street. The flexibility gives him great "feel" when stalking, and the rubber keeps the foot fairly dry, and scent to a minimum.

I've also hunted with him when he's worn mid-calf brain-tanned Indian moccasins. A thin sole and being able to feel the ground are important in still-hunting. When a person normally just walks slowly, he places the heel down first, then rolls forward onto the ball of the foot. This normal walking pattern does not adapt well to still-hunting. First off, if the ball of the foot is planted first, the abnormal step will tend to psychologically make you aware you aren't just "walking slowly." You are placing your feet. You want to be very aware that you are placing your feet.

Secondly, because the ball of your foot is wider than the heel, you will have better balance planting the ball first. If you feel a twig underfoot, you can raise up the forward foot and replace it before the weight is distributed to it. Always have the weight planted solidly on the rear foot until the ball and heel of the forward foot are set quietly. Being conscious of planting the feet like this will automatically slow down your pace.

Because you are moving at such a slow pace, you are able to pick out the route that best suits your approach into or through an area. Keep below any ridge lines so you don't skyline yourself. Also, try to keep to the shadows as much as possible. Move from the shadow of one tree to the shadow of the next. Taking any wind into consideration first, try to keep the sun at your back. It'll help if the animal is somewhat blinded by the morning or evening sun.

Even though you try to keep the sun to your advantage, it's best to still-hunt with some kind of cap with a bill to block out any backlighting. Especially in low-light morning and evening conditions, you'll notice that if you try hunting without any bill on your hat, you'll lose a lot of detail to backlighting.

Use ground cover or brush to conceal your movements. Move up to a piece of cover, brush, or whatever, and stand behind it until you feel the coast is clear. Then slip around to the front side of the cover, remaining motionless, and use the new background as a cover.

Scrutinize everything and look for detail, but most of all, look for movement. Movement on the animal's part will be what your eye will pick up the quickest. Train yourself to look for it. Get right into the situation. Most guys tend to look too high. You want to concentrate your effort at the 30-inch height. In thick cover, or in an area that has an overstory or low browse line, squat right down and look under the normal eye level. You'll be surprised how much farther you can see in some areas by squatting down low. You have to. A man's average eye level is probably five or five and a half feet, while a deer's is only maybe three. If you don't squat down, they are going to get you before you get them.

Don't worry about the movement of squatting down. Because of a deer's eye construction, they will pick out horizontal movement much quicker than movement on the vertical plane. Your motion should be slow, just like all other movements when still-hunting, but the advantages of bending or squatting far outweigh the disadvantages of excessive movement.

If you think you hear something, stop and cup your ears. You can hear two or three times as well with your hands cupped around your ears. Don't laugh. Why do you think a deer's ears are cupped? Not to mention that they can swivel that cup and focus their hearing potential behind them. If you don't think it makes any difference, try this little experiment. Sit behind the wheel of your car with the tape deck or the radio playing normally. Then cup a hand behind each of your ears. Like my friend Pat Wolf says, "It sounds like somebody turned the volume up two decibels."

Watch your breath when you're still-hunting. First of all, if you're getting winded (out of breath) while still-hunting, you're moving way too fast. A good still-hunter should not get out of breath while climbing even the highest, steepest mountain. He should be moving too slowly to get out of breath. At any rate, the original point I was trying to stress was the fact that if you're breathing is producing visible breath or vapors, they can be detected as movement at fairly long ranges—especially if the sun is shining on the vapors. That's another good reason to keep in the shadows. Breathe through your nostrils. That will cut the noticeable vapors almost in half.

I remember one memorable stalk I pulled off about fifteen years ago while still-hunting whitetails on an island in the middle of Yellowstone River. I used to like to slip these islands because the sandy soil of the river bottom made for some exceptionally quiet walking. This one morning, I looked up and my eye caught a huge rack from a big typical buck that was bedded down behind a pile of driftwood.

The sandy soil was perfectly quiet, but it was littered with a covering of dead, dry cottonwood leaves. I had to squat down and literally clear myself out a spot to place my feet for the next step. Tension was high as I inched forward, and the rack became more enormous with each step. I was sure there was about to be an explosion of muscular power as the buck leaped from his bed. I was going to snap shoot an arrow through his lungs before his front hoofs hit the ground on the initial lunge.

But the great bound never came. I felt like an idiot when I got close enough to realize it was not a buck I was stalking after all, but a shed antler that had been washed atop the pile of driftwood during the spring floods. It had just coincidentally settled perfectly upright into a position that had the appearance of a bedded buck behind the driftwood. I've kept that shed antler to this day to remind me of the experience. Given a 20-inch inside spread, the deer would have just squeaked into Boone and Crockett.

As I said earlier, when it comes to producing trophies, still-hunting is more conducive to the rifle hunter than the bowhunter. No matter how careful and how sneaky you might think you are, a good mature buck will usually catch you off-guard before you catch him. If you've done everything else right, he may spook, run out a short ways, and stop long enough to make a decision. This short length of time often is enough for an alert rifle hunter to drop the deer on the spot. But alas, the poor bowhunter usually stands there with the frustration of the deer out of range, and the entire area on red alert. And that's usually the majority of the time. But when everything goes just right—that one time in dozens when all the cards fall just the way you want them to—that's when the challenge and thrill of the experience matches or equals most any one-on-one hunting experience you'll ever come up against.

9

Going to the Boneyard

By John Trout, Jr.
(Spring 2002)

Like any avid deer hunter, I fight it to the finish. First comes early archery, then firearm, blackpowder, and late archery seasons. I'm obsessed with finding and hunting crafty whitetails. But that's not to say that I hang up my boots and dwell on past hunts while waiting several months for a new season to begin. On the contrary, I avoid post-season depression by shed hunting. And sometimes this invigorating pastime puts me onto a big buck for the fall.

There is satisfaction in finding a shed antler simply because it is yours to own and admire (subject to state and provincial laws on picking up sheds). No two are identical. It is also fun to study the antlers closely and learn something about the genetics of deer roaming your area. However, there's another good reason for shed hunting.

First, consider that any shed antler found in your area provides positive proof of a buck that survived the previous hunting season. Shed hunting is a way to determine your chance of locating a trophy buck when

Bucks don't care where or when they shed their antlers. Some may lose half their headgear a few days before the other half falls off. Most bucks lose both sides within a few hours, however. *Credit: John Trout Jr.*

the hunting begins. Even a shed from a yearling buck provides evidence that a 2½-year-old buck might be in the area when the season opens.

Shed hunting is more than a casual walk through the woods. You could find old rub and scrape lines that you never knew existed. Providing you know and understand white-tailed buck habits, you will have good opportunity to find sheds and the past season's rut sign.

First Things First

If you begin looking too early or too late in the post-season, you will probably find nothing and get bored. Be mindful that, as sunlight decreases in the late winter months, a buck's testosterone level drops and causes his antlers to shed. Some bucks shed as early as late December, while others don't shed an antler until April. Most individuals who consistently hunt for sheds usually begin after most of the bucks have shed. Throughout much of North America, the majority of the bucks will have shed their antlers by late March. Mature bucks shed their antlers before the young bucks do (although exceptions do occur).

I begin spending time in the field toward the end of February. However, I locate most sheds in March. I have also found numerous sheds in April while turkey scouting and hunting. But be aware that shed antlers have a way of disappearing quickly in some regions. Many critters, including squirrels, mice, and rabbits, love to gnaw on the discarded bone. How fast an antler vanishes depends on how quickly animals find it. I have found sheds in the fall that were only slightly gnawed, while others that I stumbled onto in June and July while hunting woodchucks were chewed down to practically nothing.

Once you begin shed hunting, be prepared to cover plenty of ground. Consider, too, that many bucks that roamed your area during the hunting season are now tucked away in the freezer. Yes, looking for a shed antler is like looking for the proverbial needle in a haystack. However, the right timing, coupled with knowing where to look, certainly helps.

Feeding Areas vs. Bedding Areas

A white-tailed buck does not care where he sheds his headgear. You could find sheds in both feeding zones and bedding zones, as well as along trails. I'll get around to walking trails in just a moment, but first, let's look at feeding and bedding areas. Bucks spend much of their time in these two areas in the post-season.

Most shed hunters claim they find the majority of their sheds in feeding areas, primarily agricultural fields and pastures where the bucks spend their time in the dark hours. However, I believe that just as many antlers are shed in and near bedding zones. You won't find as many sheds in bedding areas as you do in feeding zones, though, because they are harder to see. Even a pure white antler has a way of vanishing before the eyes of an observant shed hunter who passes by it a few feet away. Obviously, the denser the area, the more difficult the antler will be to find.

I have often spotted sheds in open fields from long distances. Binoculars come in very handy, but footwork is still required if you hope to be successful. When hunting for sheds in bedding zones, cover ground slowly and cautiously. You'll spend more time here than you will searching for sheds in feeding areas. Also, never assume that an antler will be totally visible. I have found some only because I saw the tip of a point protruding out of debris. I have also found antlers that were hanging on limbs about waist-high. When the antlers loosen, bucks will attempt to remove them with their hooves, or by scraping them against the ground or limbs.

If you simply want to find sheds for the sole reason of locating a buck that you want to hunt, feeding areas are good places to spend your time carefully walking and searching. Fields are also prime areas to locate the most sheds if you are simply interested in owning and admiring antlers.

On the other hand, you should consider finding bedding areas. During late winter, deer spend much of their time in the bedding areas, reserving body fat. Thus, it is common for a buck to rise out of his bed on a cold afternoon and knock off a loose antler. You might also learn the whereabouts of a big buck's hideout and home range, and connecting trails that will lead you to old rutting sign that could soon become fresh pre-rut sign.

Trail Pursuits

I love walking deer trails, particularly those that connect to dense bedding areas. I often start in the thickest locations and search for trails leading into them. I spend some time searching the bedding area for sheds, but quickly resort to following the trails.

Now, you might be wondering if spooking deer will hurt your upcoming hunting season. It is true that you will send deer running and leave human scent behind. But it won't hurt your hunting, since several months elapse before the season opens. Any disturbance you make is sure to become history to even the wisest bucks.

Trails found along fencelines, ditches, and other natural travel corridors offer the best opportunities to find sheds. Trails that seem to meander forever through hardwoods seldom produce much action. One proven practice is to walk the feeding areas and look for sheds, then begin walking the trails that lead to the food sources and bedding areas. A given trail might not get used heavily during the post-rut, but this can be determined by locating fresh sign. Don't be discouraged, though, if you find trails that are not riddled with tracks and sign during late winter and early spring while you hunt for sheds. You might not find any sheds, but these trails could lead you to seasoned rub lines and scrapes that will be opened during the hunting season. A return visit in the fall could paint an entirely different picture of a trail that isn't being used during the period when bucks shed their antlers.

When shed hunting, I enjoy walking trails more than feeding and bedding areas. I don't find many sheds along trails, but it is the best way to locate old scrape- and rub lines. Walking trails, however, might also be the best way to find a matched set of antlers.

Last year while walking a trail, I located both antlers of a 10-pointer that were shed only a few feet apart. Finding a matched set is rare. Most bucks will shed both of their antlers within a few hours of each other, but this does not make the task of finding a matched set any easier. A buck can cover a lot of ground in a short time, and the shed hunter must be prepared to do the same if he hopes to find a match.

Fortunately, it is not necessary to find a matched set of sheds in order to locate a buck to hunt. One antler is all it takes to know that a big buck exists. You also know that the future headgear he carries will probably be larger than the shed antler you located. Walking trails, particularly before the spring foliage has sprung, provides you with a good understanding of the trails in your area and the bucks using them. You might find sheds and see obvious sign made during the previous hunting in the rut.

The Puzzle

Okay, so you find the shed of a monster buck along a certain trail, in a feeding or bedding zone. What does this tell you? After locating a shed, I assume that the buck will not be in the same area when the rut arrives a few months later. However, I do assume that the buck will be there during the pre-rut period. Since most bucks shed their antlers after the rut has subsided, and have returned to their home range before shedding, one can bet that they will be somewhere in the area during the early hunting season before the rut.

Since shed hunting might also put you onto rubs and scrapes, you can assume that these locations will become valuable ambush sites during the pre-rut and rutting periods.

One example of this took place a couple of years ago when I located a rub line along a creek in a dense thicket. Several huge, scarred trees indicated the rub line was active year after year. I returned to the creek and hung a treestand just before the peak of the rut the following season. The second time I was there, a huge 8-pointer passed within range. Unfortunately though, my arrow passed just under the buck's brisket and I was left wondering how I missed the 25-yard shot.

It is downright tough to scout for trophy bucks, or any buck for that matter, during the hunting season. Hotspots are easily located during the hunting season, but our presence and disturbance can promptly spoil an upcoming hunt. Scouting during the post-season, however, eliminates a lot of footwork that is usually necessary when it comes time to choose and set up an ambush site during the season. In fact, setting up a treestand several months in advance is not a bad idea.

Shed hunting could become your favorite outdoor pastime, and it will make your deer hunting more enjoyable and rewarding. I have found four good reasons for shed hunting: (1) I always need the exercise; (2) Late winter and early spring are good times to look for valuable deer sign; (3) I will be one step ahead of other hunters; and (4) I can pick out the buck I want to shoot long before the hunting season begins. Shed hunting is an excuse to get these things done!

10

The Science Of Hunting Points

By Brad Herndon
(Hunting Annual—1994)

Huge rub trees and massive scrapes draw treestand hunters like a magnet draws metal. Quantities of whitetail hunters also flock to well-worn deer trails, especially those passing through funnels and other strategic locations. Those are good hunting locations, and some good deer are taken there, but in spite of this intelligent pursuit on the hunters' part, trophy bucks continue to escape year after year in some locations. Why is this? I can tell you why. Trophy bucks are smart. When an influx of deer hunters invade their domain, they employ every survival tactic they know, including the cunning use of points. Yet points are tremendously under-hunted and little understood, a problem I hope to help alleviate.

Hunting a lowland point helped hunter Jon Davidson take this 17-pointer with a shotgun. *Credit: Brad Herndon*

A dozen years of studying points have revealed to me some astonishing secrets about trophy whitetails. These I gladly share for your information, experimentation, and evaluation.

Although points differ in height, length, and width to a vast degree, I separated them into two categories: lowland points and hardwood hills points.

Lowland Points—Discreet, but Dynamite

Lowland points are discreet, subtle, inconspicuous, indistinct, and low-profile. Just as one might expect, then, they are almost always overlooked—by the hunter, that is, not the deer. More often than not, these points are associated with, or formed by, rivulets, streams, lakes, rivers, or swamps. At times, buster bucks ingeniously use these small points to avoid hunters, moving between them completely unobserved. Here's an example of how they pull this off.

In 1978, I was drawn to bowhunt in the Indiana Army Ammunition grounds at Charlestown, Indiana. This restricted zone had not been hunted for years, and it was quite common to see between 50 to 100 stunted deer out in the pasture fields as the bus took you to your assigned hunting area. From these pasture areas, small streams trickled down short gullies, forming larger streams in the small valleys below that emptied into the adjacent Ohio River.

Seeing deer was no problem, but bagging one was a lot harder. Many of the does and fawns stayed out in the middle of the pastures. Smart thinking, really. It was quite humorous to see bowhunters chase them futilely back and forth all day. The bucks, of course, stayed in cover, so that's where I hunted. It was an eerie hunt because a browse line (something I had never seen before) separated the foliage above from a bare forest floor below. Occasionally, while still-hunting, I would catch a glimpse of antlers filtering away from me. Sadly, as the setting sun brought the day to a close, success had eluded me.

Despite not getting a deer that day, I gained a lot of knowledge, most of it concerning lowland points. As I mentally reconstructed the day's hunt, I took note of the stand location of most hunters. The majority of hunters were either positioned in the woods at the edge of the pastures, or in the forested valleys below. Both placements contained heavily used trails, as well as numerous scrapes and rubs, all indicators of hotspots.

Intriguingly, the area between the pastures above and the valleys below contained no hunters. Actually, that terrain was a series of small points lying side by side like fingers, which had been formed by the rivulets (or small streams) as they gradually dropped to the valley below. There were deer trails on the tops of these points, most of which had been walked by humans going back and forth between the pastures and the valleys. I suspected then that the bucks were using those small points to avoid hunters by traveling in a direction running perpendicular to the length of the points.

That way, all they had to do was ease over the side of the point if a hunter came along the top, or even move over to the next point, if need be. I decided right then that if I had the opportunity to hunt the region again, I would take a stand midway between the pasture and the valley, on top of one of those small lowland points.

I was in luck. The next year, 1979, I was drawn again to bowhunt the Charlestown Powder Plant facility. Even better, I was assigned the exact area I desired to hunt. Well before darkness lifted, the old bus dropped me off by a gunpowder bunker and I slowly walked down a point, my flashlight beam searching out a deer trail that traveled perpendicular to the length of the ridge.

About halfway down the point, I found a faint one. A small tree downwind of the trail, equipped with just the right amount of horizontal branches, served as a comfortable placement for me ten feet above the ground. One half-hour after daylight, I caught the movement of deer legs coming up the side of the point. Within seconds, a body materialized above those legs, carrying a good rack. I shot the 3½-year-old 8-pointer at seven yards as he crossed over the point. Short tines kept him from making Pope and Young, but at 186 pounds, field-dressed, he was hardly stunted!

That was a particularly rewarding hunt for me, because I was able to go into a trophy whitetail's domain, analyze his movement patterns, and then position myself to take advantage of what I had learned. I believe we whitetail hunters, in order to be consistently successful, must always believe we have overlooked a crucial factor, a way to make us the winner instead of Mr. Big. Consider the following situation I encountered a few years back in the infancy of my point-hunting learning process.

I was gun hunting a lowland section that contained a large forested tract several hundred acres in size. Most of this forested tract was flat and brushy, containing few distinct geographical features. Deer trails randomly meandered here and there without any pattern. At the south end of this huge brushy flat, five points, all low and gradual, snaked out into a network of fields.

Rather than lying parallel, these points lay fan-like, each leading into a central hub that I call a converging point. The deer moved naturally up and down the points since hunter pressure was very low, not forcing bucks to use the points in a perpendicular direction. The converging point was loose, with not all the trails crossing in the same spot—making it difficult to cover with a bow—but a high percentage location for a well-equipped gun hunter. When the wind was just right, I slipped downwind of the converging point one morning to observe the deer traffic that crisscrossed the hub. Even as I quietly ascended the tree, deer filtered silently by, less than 50 yards away. Intermittent deer activity kept me entertained until 9:30 a.m., when I nailed a 3½-year-old 8-pointer that was trailing a doe.

The higher percentage converging point hub had paid off, and as it so often happens, on the very first hunt. Sure, I might have bagged him in some other spot; but then again, maybe not. The configuration of the points formed a key element in the deer puzzle, a piece I used to full advantage, bringing me quick success.

Hardwood Hills Points— Neglected Hotspots

These converging points, while rather rare in lowlands, are commonplace when we start hunting the hardwood hills points, a type of terrain found in a large number of states. How well deer use these possible centers of activity depends on the drop of the points.

If the points drop off rapidly, forming a steep incline, deer usually will avoid using them because it's too much work. Instead, they will use the sides of the hills. On the other hand, if two or more points gradually slope down to feeding grounds, you can bet your boots the area where those points converge on the ridge will be a buck producer. I hunt these types of hardwood hills points quite a lot, with excellent success rates.

Now a few words regarding those deer that use the sides of the hills. In the absence of converging points in hardwood hills (an occasional occurrence), a number of solitary points may be found that run for ½ to 1½ miles or more before descending to lower elevations below. A deer trail may be found on the top of these ridges, quite frequently appearing to carry heavy deer traffic. Don't let this fool you. Deceptively, most of the time the sign looks much better than the traffic flow really warrants. More importantly, a quick walk down each side of the ridge will reveal well-worn trails running parallel with the ridge top. These are the ones bucks use most often.

If one of these side-of-the-hill trails is walked out toward the decline of the point, you will find that where the point reaches the same elevation as the side trails, the trails will cross. This means both side-of-the-hill trails, as well as the ridge trail, all come together at one spot. After they all cross, they again meander off in various directions. Obviously, this spoke-wheel-of-trails intersection is a first-rate stand site.

The just-described cloverleaf, along with the previously mentioned converging points, give the trophy hunter another critical advantage over the deer: a predictable wind movement direction. A dreaded gully, which I avoid like the plague, may throw four different wind directions at you in fifteen minutes. Even the side-of-the-hill hunting can be tough. A variable wind may produce a vacuum when it gusts over the ridge top, creating a 180-degree switch in wind direction, on and off, all day long.

The ridge top and point slopes where hotspots are found, thank goodness, are a little closer to heaven. When hunting there, once you determine from which direction the wind will blow, it will remain the same throughout the day unless extraordinary conditions exist. You will be surveying a strategic deer interchange with the wind blowing in your face all day. Who could ask for more ideal conditions than that?

Even short length, solitary points that join to a main ridge should not be overlooked when you are analyzing deer movement patterns. In fact, last year just such a formation produced one of the most interesting hunts of my deer-career.

A farmer friend of mine had found a matched set of shed antlers scoring in the 140s. This was definitely a shooter, so I decided to hunt the buck. The area near where the sheds were found contained a good saddle, one of my favorite hunting locations. I thought the big buck was in trouble . . . my first mistake.

On one of my first hunts in the low, deep-gap saddle, I had a most interesting experience. I saw a 3½-year-old buck traveling parallel to the top of a small point that jutted out from the main ridge. This surprised me, because he was up high where no trail existed. I wrote it off as a fluke occurrence. Two days later, I saw the same buck travel the same route. This time, when I left my stand, I did a fine-toothed-comb examination of the hillside. Sure enough, my probing revealed an ever-so-faint deer trail. I was onto something.

Just to the north of me was another saddle, which meant this little point projected out from the main ridge between two saddles. Immediately, I high-tailed it over the top of the point where close examination again revealed a faint trail, high up on the hillside above the other saddle. This meant a faint trail ran along each side of the short, one-eighth-of-a-mile long point, providing bucks a means of traveling through the area without getting within shooting distance of the strategic saddles.

By walking each of these faint trails, I discovered they came together where the point dropped to their elevation, just as in the long points previously discussed. As is typical, the trails fanned out again after this intersection hub. Rub trees in the area with 6-inch diameters helped me make a commitment to hunt this potential new hotspot. Four days later, when the wind was right, I made an approach up a gully and positioned my treestand where I could observe the crossing point of the faint trails. Daylight brought bad news. I had located my stand slightly too far away from the trails. After mentally complaining for three hours, I quietly dismantled my stand and began a snail-like journey up the hillside to a better location.

A deer blowing to the east on the faint trail brought me to attention. Shortly, the 3-year-old 8-pointer sighted twice previously bounded over the point barely 75 yards away, fear showing in his face. I passed the shot, knowing something bigger was behind him. Within seconds, a wild-eyed doe blasted along behind him. "Hmmm, interesting," I thought, "a doe chasing a buck." Five more minutes of observation produced no action, so I inched up fifteen more yards. Once more, movement to the east caught my eye.

Almost magically he appeared, running wide open; 10 tall tines, white in color, flashed in the sun. Being experienced in chasing does, the huge buck never came to the intersection hub. Instead, he cut over the top of the small point in hopes of intercepting the doe. I had a 100-yard shot, through timber, at a running buck that would be the fulfillment of a longtime ambition for me. I never raised the gun; the shot was risky beyond my skills.

Hunting him and learning one more of a whitetail's avoidance tricks has given me a deeper sense of awe for their marvelous intelligence. Still, there is much to learn. Take what I have written; analyze it, digest it, use it, enlarge upon it, and maybe it will help put the whitetail of a lifetime on your wall.

11

Forget About Scrapes

By Bill Winke
(October 2001)

Nothing in the deer woods captures the imagination of a hunter like a fresh bathtub-sized scrape. It creates a vision that plays like a movie in our minds. The buck's wide antlers are held low to the ground as he throws leaves and dirt ten feet behind him with each furious rake of his foreleg. His neck stretches and his back arches as he takes the overhead branch into his mouth and rubs it across his pre-orbital glands before shredding it with his antlers. It's an awesome daydream, one that makes hunters immediately begin looking for a nearby tree that's big enough to hold a treestand. But turning the dream into a reality is the tough part.

Let's look at a common mistake. When Joe Hunter thinks of the rut, he thinks of scrapes—big scrapes, small scrapes, lines of scrapes, every kind of scrape. He wants them near his stands; he wants to find them when he's scouting, and his eyes light up when he finds one "as big as the

If you think you can take a trophy like this one simply by watching a fresh scrape, you'd better think again. *Credit: Bill Lea*

hood on my Chevy." The bigger they are, the better. Well, Joe's in for a tough season. I should know; I was Joe myself once.

I learned the hard way, through several frustrating seasons, that scrapes aren't some kind of rut-hunting panacea. In fact, today I don't even look at them. I've become the Anti-Joe. I don't care if scrapes are near my stands. I don't even care if there's a single scrape on the entire farm that I'm hunting. They carry almost no information that interests me. Why? Scrape hunting simply doesn't work. Well, that might be a little strong. At least, it doesn't work the way most hunters think it should.

There are many misconceptions concerning scrapes and what they mean to deer. As a result, many hunters still sit over the wrong ones at the wrong times and eventually become frustrated. You can read volumes on scrapes and how to classify them with fancy, meaningless terms like *primary* and *secondary* and *boundary* and *edge*. In the end, there are really only two kinds of scrapes: those that will be visited again by the buck that made them, and those that won't. If you really want to put scrapes to work this fall, cut through the fog of misconception and gain a better understanding of what scrapes really mean.

Scrape Enlightenment

I grew up on a farm, and like everyone else along our road, our mailbox was at the end of the drive. It was the focal point for every dog in the neighborhood. Daily, I watched mutts stop and raise their hind leg at our mailbox post. Every time I let my own dog out of his kennel, the first thing he did was run to the mailbox. He sniffed around it for a while, and then marked the post himself. Satisfied that he was still the king of all he surveyed, he put on an impressive demonstration of grass pawing and then ran off to take care of other important business, like keeping our cats in shape.

In no way did this canine scent post serve as a means for male and female dogs to get together. I never looked out the front window to see a female bedded nearby waiting for Rover to appear. The mailbox was used only by males to keep track of other males, possibly even as a way to maintain order in the local dominance hierarchy. Scrapes serve much the same function in the whitetail world.

It is believed that scrapes communicate many different forms of information and provide a means for bucks to keep tabs on other bucks. A buck working a scrape leaves identifying scent in two ways. They leave saliva and secretions from the pre-orbital gland on the scrape's ever-present overhanging branch, and they urinate over their hock glands to leave scent in the scrape itself. It's not fully understood exactly what these scent cues mean to other deer.

It's been a long-held misconception that scrapes serve as a kind of single's bar for deer. Bucks are supposed to go there during the rut and find does waiting for them. That logic is a bit too convenient. The rut is far too chaotic in most of North America for such orderly meetings to occur. In fact, when the rut peaks and much of the doe population is either in estrus, or soon to be, bucks rarely work scrapes, and certainly don't use them as their first-line offense when looking for love. They're on the move from doe to doe and will quickly abandon rituals that take time away from their search.

Biologists now believe that scrapes might have actually run their course by the time breeding begins. According to R. Larry Marchinton and Karl Miller of the University of Georgia, "Once does begin to come into heat in large numbers, dominant bucks no longer need to advertise their availability, as they are fully occupied by breeding duties." They believe that scrapes are a means for subordinate bucks to learn whether or not a dominant buck is available in the area. If so, it is quite likely that the sexual intensity of the lesser buck is suppressed. Dominant bucks use scrapes to learn whether or not another dominant buck has moved in on their turf—throwing the local pecking order out of whack and possibly even spurring a battle. (That's why it is possible to stir up local bucks by throwing the hock gland from a dominant buck shot elsewhere into a scrape.)

It has also been theorized that estrous cycles in does might be fine-tuned by the scent they find in scrapes. Scent-posting in scrapes is a very complex process—one that still offers many more questions than answers. Fortunately, we don't need to know all the answers to figure out where and when to hunt them.

Finding the Right Scrapes

If, as today's biologists suggest, scrapes are most useful to local bucks prior to peak of breeding, then let's focus on finding the right ones and strategies for hunting them at this time. In other words, I'm going to forget about scrapes past the start of breeding, and you should, too. The following strategies apply to the period starting about two weeks before the first does begin to come into estrus. The point is to find scrapes that are likely to be visited regularly during this time.

Scrapelines are the best scrapes to hunt. They do little more than expose a buck's travel corridor, but that's valuable information. He's probably not going to come in and freshen one scrape and then leave. He's going to move all the way through as he goes from Point A to Point B. For this reason, you don't need to sit right on top of a scrape as long as you can cover the travel route the buck was using when he made it. In this way, you can better use terrain, cover, and local wind flows to your maximum advantage when setting up your ambush. Maybe you can't take him down in the draw, but you do have a chance up on the ridge where the scrape line leads.

Early pre-breeding is the best time to hunt scrape lines. This occurs just prior to the first real chasing of the rut—about two weeks before does start to come into estrus. In many parts of the continent, this is the last week of October. Bucks are still staying close to home, but are starting to move more as they check out does in feeding areas.

You should be looking for scrapelines, not just individual scrapes. This distinction is important because it affects the way you scout and hunt. Bucks don't lay out a line of scrapes and then set up a travel route to check them. It's just the opposite: bucks make scrapes along their existing travel routes—most often between bedding and feeding areas. You should already be lightly hunting these corridors anyway. The scrapes are just a bonus—confirmation that bucks are beginning to move more.

If you find a random scrape that isn't along a believable travel route, it's not all that valuable. A scrape along the edge of an open field is not the goal. However, a handful of deeply dug scrapes found back in the cover along a faint trail leading to a creek crossing, and then up a ridge to a bean field, is a much better find. There's a pretty decent chance you can tag a buck here.

You've got about a week to ten days after the scrapes become active to take the buck that's using this travel route. After that, the first hint of estrous activity in the doe herd will take him right off his pattern, and the action on these scrape lines will go down considerably.

A word of caution: Bucks love to scrape in the cool, damp earth found at the bottoms of draws and ravines. This is a great place to find sign, but a decidedly difficult place to hunt. When the wind blows, it will

More sign: Does it all add up? Is this area worth hunting? Or are the bucks just passing through here, and not spending time in the area? The smart hunter pieces all the clues together before deciding what areas to hunt.

Credit: Bill Winke

swirl here. Resist the temptation to hunt these spots, focusing instead on locations where you can better control where your scent blows.

If you are hunting travel routes, you are probably hunting scrape-lines by default as the rut approaches. I don't really call that scrape hunting. On the other hand, the real "scrape hunting" occurs when you look for, and then hunt, a single scrape.

This is the kind of low-odds strategy that turned me sour on scrape hunting. I expected bucks to show up like clockwork. It just doesn't work that way. Pinning all your hopes on one scuffed-up patch of dirt is a fairly low-odds proposition. One big scrape is alluring to a hunter, but is generally not as productive as a line of scrapes. The buck that made the individual scrape has to be so excited about the upcoming rut and determining who is the dominant stud, that he will go out of his way to check the scrape often. In some cases, it can happen, especially when these scrapes are located back in the cover near known buck bedding areas, but I'd rather spend my time on travel routes. They're more consistent.

If you're bent on being a "true" scrape hunter, the tricky part is finding these individual scrapes without putting the local buck (who is still hanging around and very sensitive to pressure) on red alert. Obviously, the best time for scouting and stand placement is after the season. These scrapes generally appear in the same location every year, giving you a good idea what will happen next season. The best time to hunt these is the period starting two weeks before the first does come into estrus.

Every year, individual scrapes pop up in another location: the bottlenecks of narrow travel funnels. Just as such locations are great places for a treestand, they are also good places for a buck to scent-check for does. Scrapes found in travel funnels are basically coincidental. You should be hunting these spots when the conditions are right, whether the scrape is there or not.

Scrapes to Avoid

During a late fall walk along the edge of the woods, you will likely notice many scrapes under overhanging tree limbs. Some of these will make your jaw drop, but scrapes made along open fields are almost always worked to their awesome size at night by several different bucks, and are rarely visited during daylight. Edge scrapes are low-odds places for an ambush.

No single hunting technique is ever going to produce king-sized bucks under all conditions, and scrape hunting is no exception. You will take more big bucks over the course of your life by focusing on how bucks relate to cover, terrain, doe concentrations, and hunting pressure than you ever will by simply sitting over a scrape. Think deeper. Scrapes are part of the overall picture, but only one small part.

12

Triple Your Deer Harvest

(With Permanent Stands and Consistent Record Keeping)

By Charles Pittman
(Spring 2000)

What a nightmare! I'm referring to bygone days when I crawled out of bed long before dawn, strapped a bulky portable stand, rifle, and other gear on my back, and headed off into the rainy South Carolina woods. Stumbling through the darkness on a particularly cold and miserable morning, my hunting companion of twenty years and I decided there had to be a better way.

Having grown up in Kansas, my friend frequently reminisced about the pleasures of hunting in permanent tower stands. His descriptions of the comfort and ability to hunt longer hours eventually persuaded our three other friends who shared the 400-acre hunting lease to build several towers. Anything had to be better than risking life and limb as we inched

83

The author and his son, Reese, took this nice 6-pointer from a power line that is always a very active morning stand. A major benefit of two-man towers is that young hunters can learn the ropes with an adult before they begin to hunt alone. *Credit: Charles Pittman*

our way up trees on shaky climbers in the rain. We wondered why any person would do this and not even get paid for the effort. It also became more difficult to answer when my wife asked why I enjoyed this more than being home with her.

It was not easy to convince our more traditional tree-climbing friends that building towers was worth the hours of extra work and added expense. Our debates were predictable: "We won't be able to get into the deep woods where the bug bucks hang out"; "What if we go to all of this trouble and the towers scare off the deer?" or "Our other hunting friends will think we've gone light in our loafers." In their eyes, one is not a real hunter unless he sits in trees, smells like a doe in heat, paints his face with camo grease, and communes with nature.

Begrudgingly, everyone agreed it was worth a try. In three years, we built thirteen fully enclosed tower stands, complete with flip-up windows and cushioned, swivel seats. On frigid days, they were even outfitted with propane heaters. Now we could drink coffee and even place our steaming cups on a small shelf if a deer appeared. We had rationalized that our primary purposes for the hunt club were friendship and camaraderie. If we were lucky, we might even shoot a few deer. But we all had serious doubts that the new stands could be productive. At best, we figured the towers would allow us to doze off and simply collapse face-first into the wall as opposed to plummeting to the ground in front of a group of snickering deer.

During our first year, we erected four towers, several large ladder stands, and donated our portable stands to anyone still crazy enough to use them. Our long-term plan was to build four towers a year until we had the accessible areas of our property covered. Within two months after first hunting from these camouflaged high-rises, we were noticing unique stand characteristics regarding deer sightings. Certain stands appeared to be better in the morning, while others seemed more productive in the afternoons.

Other stands had been disappointing during the early season, but, almost magically, became regular superhighways for deer during the colder months of November and December. Despite our instincts, everyone agreed that this was just happenstance. We felt certain that we were imagining trends when there were none.

After all, the golden rule of deer hunting is that the only times you can count on running into deer are during the rut or when they are standing next to a highway as you speed past. Other than that, they eat, sleep and roam the woods whenever and wherever hunting pressure, food sources, and their urges take them.

It was during a debate over these "presumed" trends that an idea hit me. When I suggested that we begin keeping records each time we hunted a permanent stand, my friends looked at me like I had fallen out of one too many stands, which I had. I pressed forward anyway, and developed a record-keeping notebook to be kept in the camp. It contained a tabbed section for each stand. Inside those sections, I placed a simple form on which a hunter could check off the time he had hunted, what he saw, when he saw it, the weather conditions, and the date. It also included space for all pertinent information about deer harvests, such as sex, weight, points, and age. Additionally, there was a small section for anything else the hunter wanted to write, such as turkey sightings that could come in handy during turkey season.

The first two seasons of record keeping were not easy. Remembering to fill out the forms was difficult for everyone, especially since we had no idea what the real payoff would be. I am certain that, at times, I sounded like a scolding mother reminding her children to wipe their feet before entering the house. Frequently, we had to recreate the information from the previous week after everyone forgot to record it. Almost everyone felt that the long hours alone in the stand had somehow transformed me into a hunting auditor.

It was not until the early part of our third season that something dramatic happened and caught the group's attention. Almost overnight, it became apparent that the two of us who had been studying the information and trends had seen and taken more deer than the others. They asked the natural question: "How could this happen if we all hunt the same stands? It must be luck." Our answer was, "It's not which stand you hunt; it's when you hunt the stand that counts."

After the third season, the skeptics admitted that they could no longer attribute our success to dumb luck. The numbers spoke for themselves, and they knew that we were onto something that was working. Furthermore, everyone wanted in on the secret. We all knew that the records we had been keeping and the trends that were becoming evident could increase our odds of seeing deer on particular stands.

Suspicions about certain stands suddenly became fact when we looked at the numbers and saw statistics. If you hunt stand "A" in the mornings in October, you have a 70-percent better chance of seeing deer than in the afternoons in that same stand. Or, if you want to take a doe on doe days, you should hunt stand "B" in the afternoons. If you want a buck, hunt stand "C" in the mornings in late October and early December.

Listed below are some of the actual deer sighting trends that have emerged from our five-year study in upstate South Carolina:

More than 94 percent of all deer sightings during our morning hunts were within a 20- to 30-minute period approximately two hours after sunrise (not right at daybreak, like many of the hard-core hunters insisted)!

More than 80 percent of all deer seen in the afternoons were seen during the last hour before sunset (our afternoon hunting hours have historically been from 3 p.m. until dark).

Seventy-three percent of all deer harvested by our club in 1997 were taken in the mornings, despite the fact that we spent almost as much time hunting in the afternoons. This morning number has been consistently rising for four years in a row (hunting primarily between the hours of daylight and 10 a.m.).

We also learned quickly that the weather had less to do with deer sightings than the old hunter's tales had led us to believe. We have taken deer as they stood in the pouring rain and sleet. Now we no longer keep weather information, because deer sighting trends at our club rarely hinge on weather conditions. In fact, the only weather that consistently reduces our deer sightings is high wind. Our suspicion is that the noise and movement created by the wind drastically masks the deer's ability to detect danger. As a result, they tend to lie down and wait for the wind to stop.

Our records show us which stands are the best to hunt throughout the season. Interestingly, at any given time during the season, we always have four or more of our thirteen stands that offer a 50-percent, or higher, chance of seeing deer. Amazingly, in 1997, we had two stands with more than 80-percent odds of seeing deer on any given day. Once we have filled our freezers with venison, we put guests in these stands so they can experience the thrill of seeing or getting a deer. Since we frequently have several guest hunters, we are usually hunting most of our thirteen stands. By doing this, we are assured of knowing if trends with certain historically unproductive stands are changing.

Since we record all deer sightings, we have tracked increases or decreases in bucks or does on our property. When we began recording more does, we knew we had to increase our doe harvest. We have done this for the last three years. Now our buck-doe ratio is roughly 3-to-10, while three years ago it was 2-to-15.

When deer sightings decrease at a stand, we plant food plots nearby to increase the activity. Or we might even work harder on the stand to ensure that it is quiet and not obtrusive. Occasionally, we have moved consistently poor stands to more productive areas.

We have learned that, for some reason, late November afternoon hunts are usually a waste of time. Therefore, we schedule our November weekends to hunt mornings and often leave at noon to gain brownie points at home.

Now that our planted pines are reaching heights of fifteen to twenty feet, the deer are using these forests as bedding areas. This accounts for the huge increase in morning sightings as deer move from the hardwoods into the pines. Similarly, stands on the edges of the pines are almost as productive in the late afternoon, because deer are moving back into the hardwoods to feed.

Stands overlooking clear-cuts are better cold weather stands than during the warmer, early season—especially for those bold bucks who are roaming the open areas for does.

Stands positioned next to grassy fields surrounded by hardwoods tend to be almost exclusively late afternoon, late season stands. With an abundance of acorns and other food in the hardwoods, very few deer venture into these fields except to walk the edges late in the day.

As I mentioned, we were initially quite skeptical of hunting from tower or permanent stands. Now we are firm believers in their merit.

Since we have well-established trails or roads leading to each of our stands, and we make little if any noise entering them, we occasionally take deer within five or ten minutes of arriving.

Since most morning deer sightings occur two hours after sunrise, we occasionally wait until it is full daylight to walk to our stands. This greatly reduces the noise caused by hunters stumbling over limbs, walking off cliffs, or running face-first into trees in the dark. Also, we are less likely to frighten deer with suspicious flashlight beams cutting through the forest.

Contrary to popular belief, once a tower stand has been in place for a few days, the deer will pay little if any attention. It is common for deer to walk directly under these towers. The closed-in nature of the stand dramatically reduces the chances that the deer will see movement, and it reduces the release of your scent into the woods. It is also much easier to quietly get into a shooting position in a tower stand than a portable one. We do not have to invest in expensive camouflage clothing like we did during our tree-climbing days. In fact, on a warm day in early October, you might just find us sitting in a tower in short pants, T-shirts, and tennis shoes!

Many diehard portable stand hunters think we have lost our marbles. But the proof is in the results. When we started hunting this property in 1991, with portable tree-climbers and ladder stands, we bagged only eight deer between four hunters. We were scouting long before the season, using buck lure, hunting over scrapes, and generally doing all the right things. In 1997, while hunting almost exclusively from tower stands, and frequently using our statistics to guide our stand selections, we took 31 deer. That's almost four times the number of deer we bagged in 1991. We harvested 13 bucks and 18 does in 1997. Since beginning our tower hunting, we have taken several great bucks—8-pointers in the 165- to 175-pound range. This can't be attributed simply to luck or a larger deer herd. We hunted 22 percent fewer hours than in 1991, stayed dry and comfortable, and enjoyed our time in the woods much more than those nightmarish days perched on a rickety portable stand.

Tower stands are only part of our secret. Keeping consistent hunting records and looking for trends in deer movement tells the full story. These facts convince us that we have finally proven deer are much more predictable than most hunters would ever guess.

Tower stands along edges can always produce, as hunters can watch trails leading in and out of cover, as well as open crop fields. *Credit: Charles Pittman*

13

Ten Tips for Black Powder Hunting Success

By Sam Fadala
(Hunting Annual—1994)

Success for one hunter is failure for another. It's a matter of personal expectations. Some are satisfied with a happy campout. Others have to bag game. We've all enjoyed hunts where no tag was cancelled, no camp meat brought in, no prize for the taxidermy shop earned, no meat for the freezer. Some hunters consider this experience at the top of the scale, showing ultimate maturity. I've never become that consummate outdoorsman, I guess. I like to smell sagebrush, listen to squirrels chattering in the treetops, watch a sunset flow red over the horizon, and enjoy the warmth of a campfire and friendship. But put a big hunk of venison, well-laced with condiments and carefully "larded," over hot coals, and the scene brightens for me. In short, I buy big game tags to fill 'em if I can, with modern rifle, bow, or muzzleloader. Maybe you're the same way: happy to build outdoor memories, but a little more jolly about the whole thing when your smokepole goes "Boom," and a harvest is yours. If you're that kind of black powder hunter, here are ten tips for success.

FIRST, carefully choose that black powder rifle (let's save big-game black powder sidearms for another time). You are no better than your "shootin' iron" when the moment of truth is hot on the air. If you can't hit a barn door, from inside the barn, you have little chance for the kind of success that comes from tagging game with a muzzleloader. Not that long ago, black powder rifle selection was simple. Today, there are more types to choose from. But believe this: Nobody but you can decide on your special sootburner. Long, short, light, heavy, old-time style, modern muzzleloader, whatever, the choice must be yours. Base that selection on what suits you best, within the parameters of legality for your particular hunt.

For example, scope sights may be taboo for your black powder season. Certain modern muzzleloaders may not be allowed. In a few rare cases, you'll need a flintlock. Otherwise, buy what fits you and your needs. Obviously, this first rule deserves a full article in itself, but we have other trails to walk. So think it over: Does your black powder rifle work for you? Can you put five shots into the bull at 100 yards with it? Is it comfortable to carry, and to shoot? You must answer yes to these questions. If you cannot, start looking for a new muzzleloader tomorrow.

SECOND, go for caliber. Black powder rifles do not gain high velocity in modern terms. For power, you must go with bullet mass. Calibers .40 and .46 are fine for conicals, but round ball shooters should look to .50s and .54s for greater punch and ultimate harvesting success. And sight in, please. Start at 13 yards. This gives you a chance to get centered on the bull's-eye at very close range; plus, normal muzzleloader trajectory puts your round ball or conical back on target at about 75 to 100 yards, with an initial 13-yard zero.

THIRD, choose the rest of your gear as carefully as your rifle. Scritchy-scratchy clothing that sings out "Here I come!" when you still-hunt is the song of failure. I realize that no one, including Hiawatha, can truly trace a path in big-game country with total silence. But give me something like a good quality fleece, or similar soft stuff, plus footgear that didn't belong to Dr. Frankenstein's monster, and I'll get a lot closer to game. So will you. So, buy hunting garb with quiet in mind, because

91

Practicing with natural rests is a good, realistic way to gain confidence in your shooting. *Credit: Russ Thornberry*

black powder is a game of close-shooting, and getting close means keeping the noise down.

FOURTH, practice with your rifle, not always from the bench, but also from normal field stances. Especially, practice field rests. If you hunt open terrain, try a walking staff to steady your rifle. When hunting with partners who also use hiking staffs, learn to cross two sticks for a steadier standing shot. If the stick is not your bag, rest your rifle over a log, or pad a boulder and plant the forearm. Shoot standing, too, with the rifle you plan to carry in the field. Learn to hold a precise sight picture with irons, open or peep. And if open or aperture sights are not for you, mount a scope on your firebreather, provided the law allows, and a scope suits your sense of black powder propriety. In short, learn to "shoot good" with that black powder rifle.

FIFTH, after your rifle is tuned, tune yourself. This means honing your senses. The concrete walls of civilization give us a great many amenities, but city life also robs us of our natural abilities. For example, we're not hound dogs, but our noses aren't useless, either. One day I caught a whiff of something that smelled like elk, but I was in the badlands and elk were probably no closer than 50 miles away. I kept my head into the wind and slowly followed my olfactory machine a step at a time. I came upon four deer feeding in a draw. None was a buck. Nonetheless, I'd sniffed out game. Eyes and ears are even more important. It's mostly a matter of remembering that human senses can be fine-tuned to work better in the outdoors, even when suppressed daily from bombardment of city life.

SIXTH, learn the lay of the land. Scout it out. And if you need help, get it. I'm not embarrassed to admit that I have a little network going for me much of the time, including other hunters, ranchers, and many outdoorsmen who are active where I hunt. I make contact with these guys from time to time for a report. When they tell me game is here, not there, I listen, and then I scout it out for myself. The black powder hunter is handicapped on purpose. He likes it that way, but he must also take advantage of opportunities when they come, and the more opportunities the better. Scouting and learning a territory pays off big, increasing those opportunities.

SEVENTH, stay a while if you can. Nothing beats skill in woodsmanship, knowing the quarry, being able to find and get close to big game. However, Lady Luck is never very far away from anybody who calls himself a big-game hunter, and one way to improve luck is sticking around a while. That's because time creates more of those opportunities mentioned earlier. You don't have to backpack into the outback, although hoofing it beyond the main trail can often put you into quiet places just right for smokepole hunting. Take your travel trailer, truck camper, or make a tent camp—just stay a while. And cover some ground. Going slowly promotes quietness, I know, but sometimes there is no substitute for covering a patch of territory. It's a matter of odds. Odds are, the more tiny niches you see, the better your chance of running into game.

EIGHTH, magnify your view. This is especially important in open terrain; but I've hunted the woods of Alabama, and I've trod trails in Pennsylvania and New York, and everywhere I went, binoculars were a real boon. I've found more big game with glasses, especially in mountain and plains territory. But even in the brush and woods, I spotted more game with binocs than the naked eye alone ever showed me. Get the best binocs you can afford, and learn to find game with them. This means getting steady and studying every patch of geography, looking not for a big old buck standing out like a red blister on a clown's nose, but rather a piece of a deer or other game animal, a glint of eye, a bit of hide, a white rump patch, a bony antler. Make yourself an expert at finding game with the glass. The black powder hunter who finds game before the game sees him has won half the battle.

NINTH, hunt small game and varmints, such as jackrabbits, prairie dogs, and other non-game animals, with your muzzleloader at ranges up to 125 yards. Head shots only on anything edible! The transfer value from small game or varmint to big game is immense. Obvious is firearm mastery. Not so obvious is the rest of the story. Learn what to carry and how to carry it for black powder shooting success. Try out various items of new clothing, from hats to boots, checking on all manner of hardware from readyloads to cappers.

TENTH, get with the modern program. This means employing all the good stuff available to hunters these days. Using a treestand isn't cheating, you know. If stands work in your area, try one. Use a ground blind, too. Don't forget lures and scents, especially when on stand. A rag laced with lure can hold a buck's attention long enough to provide that one perfect black powder shot. Blend while still being seen with hunter's orange. Be safe, of course, but no sense standing out in plain sight, or blasting over ridges like a two-legged tank. Staying still can be a great boon to the black powder hunter. I've had deer and other big game walk right by me, even though I was not truly hidden, because I did not move. So be aware of motion.

Carry wind detection powder. Simple archery glove powder will do. It really lets you know where the wind is coming from, and just how it's behaving so you can still hunt or stalk for a close shot. Calls are also important to smokepole hunters, often serving to bring game into black powder range. Remember that most of these hunter's aids are, in theory, older than black powder itself, so don't consider them too modern for old-style hunting. They are not. Native Americans used lures and calls before the white man set foot on this continent.

Our tour on the trail of ten tips for black powder hunters ends at the fork in the trail ahead, but the story has just begun. A hunter chooses black powder for a variety of reasons—from extra opportunity, to more propitious seasons, to added challenge, historical interest, firearm knowledge, doing something the old way, and more. Range is limited, and most rifles (though not all) offer just one shot before they must be reloaded. But in spite of the handicap, the wise black powder hunter can still harvest big game. Providing meat for the table with a rifle from the past is quite a thrill. You can do it if you get a rifle that suits your style. Master that rifle, and pay attention to a few tips for success.

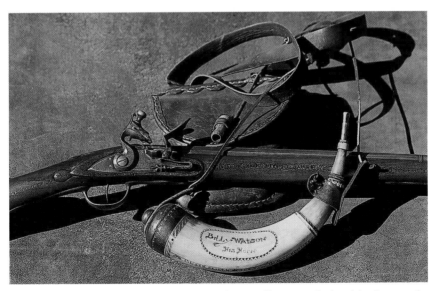

A gun, powder horn, and possibles bag—all part of the black powder hunter's wares. *Credit: Russ Thornberry*

14

Bow Tuning Made Easy

By Chuck Adams
(Hunting Annual—1994)

If you've never shot a well-tuned bow, you cannot possibly imagine what you're missing. When arrows leave a bow without wobbling, they fly with noticeably superior accuracy. If you are a decent archery shot to begin with, arrows almost seem to guide themselves to the target. Minor shooting mistakes don't dramatically affect tuned-up accuracy. An untuned bow amplifies small shooting inequities; a well-tuned setup is forgiving of minor problems. In the deer woods, where shooting is less controlled than on the target range, accuracy forgiveness can be a godsend.

Adjusting your bow and arrow for perfect flight has notable fringe benefits. Penetration in game improves, because an arrow strikes with all energy directly behind the broadhead. Bow noise subsides, because arrows absorb greater energy and pass the bow handle and arrow rest without collision. Broadheads fly well, and hit quite close to field points and other arrowheads of the same weight. Once you have shot a correctly tuned hunting bow, you will never settle for less.

Once you have shot a correctly tuned hunting bow, you will never settle for less. *Credit: Buckmasters*

Choose The Proper Ammo

Several dozen hunting arrow sizes are sold through archery stores. Most are made of top-grade tubular aluminum. A few of the lighter offerings are composed of tubular carbon. For best accuracy, most serious deer hunters use medium-weight aluminum arrows weighing 500 to 550 grains. Top grade aluminum shafts like the Easton XX75 are guaranteed straight within .004 inch, and possess uniform nock tapers and precise threaded arrowhead inserts up front. Such consistent manufacture enhances accuracy. So does the moderate 200 to 230 feet per second produced by a 60- or 65-pound hunting bow, and arrows of medium weight. If shafts are crooked or fly too fast, accuracy with big-game broadheads tends to be second-rate.

The first step in tuning is matching your bow with quality shafts of proper size. Only a handful of the forty-odd hunting shafts sold today can be made to fly accurately from your bow, so haphazard arrow selection is a mistake. You must deliberately choose the proper size, or suffer horrendous inaccuracy afield.

Fortunately, arrow shaft selection is easy. Simply consult a shaft selection chart at your local archery store, plugging in crucial factors like your personal draw length, the draw weight of your bow, and the weight of your favorite deer broadheads. The chart will probably recommend two or three feasible choices: a heavy arrow for animals over 500 pounds, a medium-weight arrow for general purpose hunting, and a lightweight shaft for extra-flat trajectory in semi-open terrain. As mentioned before, most whitetail hunters opt for middle-weight arrows.

Proper Arrow Setup

Whether you buy ready-made arrows or assemble your own from scratch, ammo must be designed for tip-top accuracy. This means three 5-inch plastic vanes or four 4-inch plastic vanes at the rear. Fletching must spiral about one degree to rotate the arrow in flight and ensure broadhead stability. Some factory-assembled arrows do not possess fletching large enough or spiralled enough to stabilize big-cutting deer broadheads. Be sure to measure fletching length before you buy arrows, and double-check fletching angle with an inexpensive plastic protractor available at any stationery store.

Every part of an arrow must be aligned to ensure good flight. It's a good idea to buy shafts guaranteed for minimum straightness and uniform nock tapers. Precision can be monitored on the rollers of an arrow-straightening tool, but it's easier to purchase top grade shafts with a long-standing reputation for uniformity. Ask your dealer for ammo recommendations.

How a nock snaps to the bowstring can make or break the bow tuning process. For best accuracy, an arrow should snap to the string, hang freely without falling off, yet be easily disengaged with a moderate finger tap to the rear of the nock. Nocks that grip the bowstring like death or slide on loosely will hinder tuning and field accuracy.

One other note on arrow setup for bow tuning. All arrowheads should weigh within five grains to ensure consistently good arrow flight. For example, all my field points, practice blunts, Judo points, and broadheads weigh 150 grains, and all fly to identical point of impact from my favorite deer-hunting bows.

Before you begin the bow tuning process, be sure your field points match broadhead weight exactly.

Basic Bow Setup

Prior to tuning, your bow must be set up exactly as you expect to hunt. Any change in the bowstring, silencers, string peep, bow quiver, bowsight, stabilizer, draw weight, draw length, arrow rest, or other bow related factors is likely to throw the bow out of tune. Outfit the bow for hunting first; then proceed with the tune.

Some bow setups are naturally more accurate than others. A bow stabilizer attached to the front reduces handle torque (twist) during a shot, and thus improves arrow flight. If you tend to grab or grip the bow too tightly as you release the arrow, a wrist sling and a wide-open bow hand will probably help you shoot.

Many modern bowhunters have discovered that non-bow quivers like a hip quiver or back quiver also improve accuracy compared to using a bow-attached quiver. A bow quiver is handy, but unbalances a bow, increases handle torque during a shot, and changes bow mass as you strip more and more arrows from the quiver. All these factors can scatter arrows to left or right of the target.

If you're serious about pinpoint accuracy on deer, you should consider a stabilizer, wrist sling, and non-bow quiver.

Arrow rest design is a standard subject of debate among avid archers. However, certain facts are indisputable.

If you prefer to draw and release the bowstring with your fingers, as approximately 50 percent of modern bowhunters do, you will need some sort of side control rest for good accuracy. An arrow bends from side to side when released with fingers, and the arrow rest must cushion and control this oscillation. Excellent side control arrow rests for hunting include the springy rest, flipper/plunger combination rest, and Cavalier Super-Flyte rest. All are horizontally adjustable—a must for easy tuning.

Most hunters who shoot with a mechanical bowstring release prefer some sort of Vlauncher or two-prong launcher rest. PSE, Martin, Golden Key, and others sell many models of this variety. Launcher-type rests are not suitable for a finger release, because they cradle the arrow from below and offer no side control. An arrow released with a trigger device does not bend dramatically from side to side, so side control is unimportant. You will need one other bit of gear to ensure a proper tune. This is a clamp-on nocking point (nock locator) for the bowstring. By loosening, sliding, and re-locking this locator with inexpensive nocking point pliers, you can eliminate vertical arrow wobble during the bow tuning process.

Bow Tuning Basics

The object of tuning is to achieve perfect, non-wobbling arrow flight from the instant the arrow leaves the bowstring. Arrow wobble causes broadheads to veer, invites fletching or shaft collision with the bow, and otherwise disrupts pinpoint shooting.

For the average hunter, so-called "paper tuning" works extremely well. To paper tune your bow, you will need a large rectangular wooden picture frame or homemade wooden frame measuring about 22x26 inches. This should be propped upright about three feet in front of a straw bale, ethafoam butt, or another dependable arrow backstop. Using thumbtacks or tape, tightly stretch and affix a single sheet of newsprint across the frame. You are now ready to shoot your bow . . . almost.

First, though, you should make sure the nocking point is affixed to the bowstring about ⅜ inch above right angles to the arrow rest. This place-ment can be achieved with a common carpenter's square, or better yet, with an inexpensive bowstring square available at your archery store. To shoot, you should always nock your arrows directly beneath this nocking point.

Stand about six feet in front of the tuning frame, and shoot a field-point tipped arrow (never a broadhead) through the newspaper. The pro-jectile will leave a telltale tear. If your bow is perfectly tuned (something that never occurs by accident), the arrow will rip a small, concentric hole in the paper with fletching marks fanning outward equally on all sides. A small, uniform tear indicates that the arrow flew with very little wobble. This ensures good accuracy with all arrowheads of the same weight.

Two types of arrow wobble show up during paper tuning. Porpois-ing, or up-and-down wobble, creates a tail-high or tail-low tear through the paper. Fish-tailing, or side-to-side wobble, creates a tail-right or tail-left tear through the paper. Most commonly, these two forms of wobble occur together, creating a diagonal tear. For example, your first shot through paper might rip tail-high and right.

The object of paper tuning is to completely eliminate oblong paper tears.

You should always correct tail-high or tail-low tearing first. If arrows tear tail-high, move your nocking point down until tearing is strictly horizontal. If arrows tear tail-low, move your nocking point up. By shooting repeatedly and experimenting with nocking point location, you can quickly eliminate porpoising arrow flight.

Next, you must adjust your arrow rest to eliminate fishtailing. If arrows tear tail-right, move the rest to the right. If arrows tear tail-left, move rest to the left. These same instructions work for both left-hand and right-hand shooters. Most commonly, a few horizontal rest adjustments will make paper tearing disappear.

If simple rest adjustment does not correct fishtailing arrows, several alternate tuning techniques might work. To eliminate tail-right paper tears, you can also: (1) increase your bow's draw weight; (2) decrease the spring tension in a springy or cushion plunger rest; (3) increase arrowhead weight; or (4) switch to an arrow shaft of weaker spine after consulting a shaft selection chart. The foregoing procedures must be reversed if you are a left-hand shooter.

To eliminate tail-left paper tears: (1) decrease your bow's draw weight; (2) increase the spring tension in a springy or cushion plunger rest; (3) reduce arrowhead weight; or (4) switch to an arrow of stiffer spine. Reverse these procedures if you are a left-hand archer.

With some diligent tinkering, you should be able to achieve small, concentric arrow tears through paper—the sign of a well-tuned bow.

Common Tuning Problems

Most modern arrow rests are well-designed, and produce excellent arrow flight when installed according to factory instructions. However, arrow fletching will occasionally collide with a rest and cause chronic wobble. If arrows persist in tearing erratic holes in paper, fletching collision may be the culprit.

To check for fletching collision, simply dust your arrow rest with talcum powder. Shoot once, and inspect the rest for places where the powder has been scuffed away.

If fletching is hitting the arrow rest or bow handle, the solution is rotating arrow nocks to change bow-to-fletching orientation. This requires

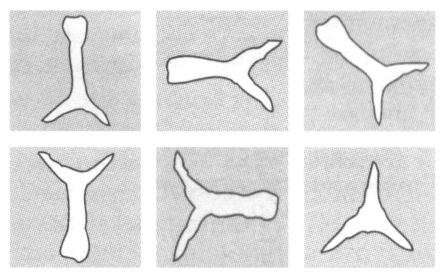

Top, from left: tail low, tail right, tail low and right; bottom, from left: tail high, tail left, perfect paper tune.

a modest investment in nocks and nock glue, but you really do not have a choice.

Through trial and error, accurate nock rotation can be achieved. When fletching ceases to scuff the talcum powder, arrows should tune up well.

Occasionally, no amount of nock/fletching experimentation will eliminate collision with the arrow rest. At this point, you should switch to another arrow rest style, or knuckle under and replace plastic fletching with feathers. Feather fletching is noisy, fragile, and prone to soak up moisture, but flattens if it touches arrow rest or bow. This ensures superior accuracy when all else fails.

Another bow-tuning culprit is loose or bulky upper-body clothing. If the bowstring even lightly brushes your chest or forearm during a shot, the arrow will veer to the left or right and wobble dramatically. This phenomenon is especially common in cold deer-hunting weather, because you must bundle up to stay warm. If you succeed in tuning your bow in thin summer clothes, you should paper test the same setup while wearing your heaviest whitetail duds. Arrows might suddenly rip paper tail-right or tail-left.

The way to eliminate clothing-caused arrow wobble is not to further adjust your bow. Adjust your clothes instead. Wear a tight hunting sweater over other upper-body garb, and make sure forearm fabric is flattened with a full-sized hunting armguard. Many cold-weather deer hunters also strap on a nylon-mesh archery chest protector to compress clothing along the upper torso. Such precautions prevent bowstring interference and ensure excellent accuracy on deer.

Final Tuning Suggestions

Paper tuning is not a perfect method, because small levels of arrow wobble are sometimes hidden in the paper tear made by arrow fletching. For this reason, broadhead-tipped arrows and field point arrows do not always fly to identical points of impact. However, if you tune properly, all same-weight arrowheads should hit within a few inches at 20 yards.

If broadheads impact slightly away from field points, simply sight-in for the broadheads. If broadheads fly dramatically off-course, something is definitely wrong. Broadheads might not be correctly aligned with arrow shafts, arrows might be crooked, or perhaps you have inadvertently changed something about your shooting setup. Double-check the tune through paper, and persist until you isolate the problem.

Once you tune your bow, it is wise to lock down arrow rest adjustments and secure these with a few drops of archery fletching cement. The nocking point on the bowstring should be tightly clamped in place, and a ring of cement applied above this locator to prevent accidental movement. If you use a mechanical bowstring release, you might want to clamp another nocking point above the first for double protection against slippage.

Smart bowhunters paper check their bow and arrow periodically to counteract unforeseen problems. Nothing boosts confidence like a well-tuned, sweet-shooting bow, and nothing ruins deer season like a bow that launches wobbling, inaccurate arrows!

15

Offbeat Tactics For Big Bucks

By Bryce M. Towsley
(Hunting Annual—1994)

The old buck plodded, slow but steady, through the snow. He had played this game before and he had always won.

He knew all the tricks to shake his pursuer, but he also knew that the tricks did not always work. Darkness, though, had never failed him. All he had to do was stay ahead of the man until nightfall, now less than an hour away. Then the man with his feeble eyesight would be forced to give up his chase.

When the snow was soft and as soundless as it was today, the hard part was telling just how far the man was behind him. But this one was different. He made a strange noise as he walked, and it was easy to pinpoint

Sometimes you have to use tactics that are a bit out of the ordinary to take bruisers such as this one. *Credit: Bryce Towsley*

his location. Suddenly, the old buck sensed something was wrong. The noise was still there well behind him, but something wasn't right.

A moment later, he collapsed in his tracks.

My grandfather's old Winchester .45-70 often had that effect on what it hit.

For this old buck, it would now be an easy winter.

The locals thought the buck was invincible. They would see him throughout the summer in the fields, but by November he would be deep in the mountains. Many tried, but nobody had been able to hang him on the game pole. He was, at least in this small Vermont farming community, a legend.

The old buck was used to being tracked by hunters, and he knew just what to do to stay out of shooting range until he could lose them. My grandfather and his brother had both been frustrated more than once by this deer, and they wanted a rematch.

They knew that with this buck's experience and intelligence, they would need a new strategy if they were to succeed. One day they came up with an idea. They had an old sleigh bell with a loop welded on it that they hung on their dog's collar so that they could keep track of him while rabbit hunting. They pinned this bell to my great-uncle's pants leg, and set out on the buck's track.

Having tracked this deer before, they knew that as long as he could hear them, the buck would soon settle into a state of cautious complacency, staying just far enough ahead, for how ever long it took. When that happened, Gramp's brother stayed on the track at the same steady pace letting the bell betray his location. Gramp, on the other hand, started circling ahead of the buck, trying to set up an ambush. Armed with a knowledge of the land, it only took a couple of tries before the buck was his, and a legend was ended.

They went on to double-team several more bucks with this method in the years ahead, but to those that laughed the first time, they never revealed the secret. When the conventional wisdom of whitetail hunting is not filling your tags, perhaps you need to try something different—maybe different enough to be called bizarre by some. Let the skeptics scoff if they will, but you might be laughing all the way to the check station.

Two decades ago, who would have thought we would be paying $10 an ounce for animal body fluids and then pouring them out to attract more critters? Could you have pictured yourself sitting in the woods grunting like a pig ten years back? Banging deer antlers together would have brought howls of laughter in my grandfather's deer camp, and a climbing treestand was as outlandish as landing men on the moon.

All these tactics were once thought of as bizarre, yet most of us use them successfully each year. An open mind was all that was needed to bring them to mainstream success. Keep yours open and read on! With Gramp's tactic, you must be hunting in the north where snow is common, and you must be hunting where there are large expanses of woods with little hunting pressure. The last thing you need to do is to run your buck into someone else to shoot.

Two men who hunt well together and have a good understanding of the land are required. For noise, most anything that is loud enough to hear, but is still subtle, is fine: a bell as they used, or perhaps an electronic beeper like the ones on bird dog's collars, will work well.

The secret is to have the buck identify the noise with his pursuers. When you first start on the track, you will undoubtedly jump him several times, but sooner or later he will associate the sound with you and will start to stay just far enough ahead of you to avoid detection. This may take a while, and it is up to you and your woodsmanship skills to determine when it is happening.

That's when one hunter starts moving ahead to set up the ambush. You still need to watch the wind and go carefully. It won't take too many mistakes to tip off a smart old buck, so make the first time you see him count.

Circle downwind and travel fast to get ahead of the buck. When you think that you are far enough ahead, cut across and look for his tracks. If he hasn't passed, stop and wait at a likely place. If you miss, try again.

If the conditions are right, and you are good, you can sometimes sneak ahead on the track and catch up with the buck. You must move fast, but quietly, and you must not miss seeing the deer. That all may sound easy, but believe me, it's not. Each of these things are relatively easy by themselves, but to do all three with zero mistakes is not a simple undertaking.

This one may never catch on with the mainstream hunters, but for the ones daring enough to try it, there might be some big bucks in the forecast.

There is an old apple orchard a mile from my house that in most years is full of deer. The trouble is that at times, it's full of hunters as well. Not just deer hunters, but bird hunters, squirrel hunters, and turkey hunters. The deer know the game. They have been playing it for years; so I use some tricks to set me apart from the herd.

Years ago the entire orchard was fenced in a feeble attempt to keep the deer out. This fence, like the orchard, has long been abandoned, and the deer have holes throughout the perimeter. I often hunt one small segment of the orchard. This is fenced on three sides and is bordered on the fourth by a faint road. The deer are bedding in the steep ledges on the mountain to the east of the orchard, and feeding on the apples at night.

There are four places in this section where these deer are passing through the fence. The first is the barway at the east end of the road. I simply park my truck there. The next crossing as I move along the east side is the most heavily used, and here I placed my treestand.

On the south end there are two more holes in the fence.

Now, I have spent all my bow-hunting career trying to avoid smelling like a man. I shower each day with scentless soap, and I carefully wash my clothes and store them in plastic bags. I don't put on my rubber boots until I am in the woods, and to avoid sweating, I dress so light when walking to my stand that I sometimes reach the tree in advanced stages of hypothermia. But when I am hunting this stand, I bring along two of the stinkiest shirts I can find in the hamper. I prefer something that I have worked in and really sweated up. I want the smell to be strong. I bring them in a sealed plastic bag and I hang them on the fence right at the other crossings.

These deer are used to man, and rather than panicking, they just avoid us all they can. If a crossing is "occupied," they move on to the next. Sooner or later, they get to the one I am waiting on.

My records indicate almost twice as many deer sightings on average when I am using this tactic from this stand than on the days when I don't place the shirts out. In the four years I have been hunting this stand, I have taken or missed a buck every year, usually on the first weekend.

When rifle season arrives a month later, things change. The hordes arrive, and the deer hole up to wait out the two-week season.

One hiding spot is a large swamp that borders the orchard on the south side. It is too wet and too thick to effectively still-hunt, but many try anyway. The deer are used to being rousted and won't go running off in a blind panic. Instead, they simply move around the danger, staying within the swamp, and usually go right back to the same bedding areas they left.

The deer like a place like this. It makes them feel safe, and they will be reluctant to abandon it.

I found several bedding areas within the swamp, and after choosing the one with the most sign, I placed a treestand there.

At midday, when I am sure that the deer are in their "hidey-hole," I go right in, breaking all the rules about hunting bedding areas. I make no attempt to be quiet, but instead thrash around as much as possible in the bedding area surrounding the stand. I want them to think that I am an idiot hunter trying to sneak up on them. The deer move out to safer quarters and I move quietly into my stand.

Before too long they start returning. It's not unusual to have them come back and bed in sight of my stand. The deer will move freely within this sanctuary, and if a buck doesn't show right off, he will often come visiting later.

One drawback is that I must stay until after dark so as not to tip my hand. I leave after the deer have gone into the orchard to feed. This may be as much as an hour after shooting light, and finding my way in this swamp in the dark has resulted in more than one dunking. But I'll suffer wet boots anytime if it means a buck on the game pole.

There is something to "beginners luck," and to a newcomer's technique. They often make mistakes so outrageous that the deer are not familiar with them.

Deer are used to hearing hunters as they make attempts to sneak up on them. When the leaves are dry, or the snow frozen, this is easily detected by even the hard of hearing in the herd, long before the hunter makes visual contact. The patterns are ingrained in the deer's brains now, what the "crunch, crunch, crunch" means. However, just "picking them up and laying them down" has a different sound all together. Beginners move way too fast, and mistakenly believe that covering more ground is the way to see deer. Often a deer will wait to see what is making that crazy noise. Perhaps they think it's a moose or another deer. Who knows for sure what they think? But sometimes, it will give you a shot.

One longtime member of our family's camp used a variation on this. He simply "took a walk in the woods." He made no attempt to be quiet, and he seldom varied his pace. He just walked and walked, all day, every day. He took a lot of bucks that way over the years, but don't ask me how. I haven't a clue.

Some savvy hunters keep a turkey call or a grunt in their mouth while hunting this way. By constantly calling, sometimes you can fool a buck into "just one last look." I used this tactic last fall while negotiating a thick patch of New Brunswick blow-downs. There was no way to be quiet, so I just crashed on through while grunting loudly and aggressively on a deer call. As I crashed out the other side, there were two bucks standing by a new scrape waiting for me. I would like to tell you that I took the biggest one. That was my intention, but it didn't happen. The chance was there, but I blew it and never fired a shot.

Another mistake that beginners often make is hunting the wrong places . . . wrong only in our experienced but closed minds.

A few years ago, there was a good 10-point buck hanging out in a field near my house. Everyone in the county had seen him, and some summer nights it was hard to get home with all the cars stopped along the dirt road to look at him.

Needless to say, the place was crowded opening day, but the buck was nowhere to be found.

A neighbor kid went hunting after school that Monday in a little bitty patch of woods along the small county airport. Everybody knew that no deer could hide in that pathetic little woodlot—everybody but the kid and the buck. They both had their photo in the morning edition of the local paper.

My cousin builds stands on his property that are so comfortable, he has trouble staying awake. One day as he was snoozing and snoring, a buck came along, curious about the strange noise. Phil heard him in the dry leaves, woke up, and collected the nice 4-pointer. Offbeat? You bet! Will it work again? I don't know; but if it does, I am going to market a deer call that sounds like snoring.

It won't be long until our gun season opens, so I've been putting in some scouting time at our camp. One new addition to our camp has been there as well. He's never taken a deer, but then, he's new to the sport. He asked me what I thought about the location he had picked for his opening morning stand.

It was as poor a place as I could think of on that mountain, and I said so. I asked him why he picked it, and he replied that it looked good to him. Further grilling revealed no other reason, and that looking good had nothing to do with sign, trails, scrapes, or anything else. It just looked good. He asked if he should move. I thought a moment, and told him no.

I'm betting that I'll be helping him drag a buck Saturday morning.

16

Scrape Pattern
Know-How

By Kathy Etling
(Hunting Annual—1994)

Scrapes have been analyzed, dissected, and fragmented by hunters eager to learn everything possible about this keystone behavior of white-tailed deer. Authors have written volumes while lecturers have droned at length about territorial scrapes, primary breeding scrapes, and secondary scrapes. When all is said and done, however, how many of us actually understand what's really been said and what should be done about hunting scrapes?

How many of us have wasted precious hunting time on what appeared to be a large, dank, primary breeding scrape, only to give up days later without ever seeing a deer? Well, take the time to read one last analysis of scrapes; one that doesn't bog us down with the boring details of each scrape, but rather looks at the patterns of scrapes as clues to the behavior

When you discover a fresh scrape like this, you know that a buck has been here recently. Now you have to figure out if he comes back regularly—and when. *Credit: Bob Etling*

of the individual bucks that made them. Once we can identify each buck's scrape pattern, we'll be better able to figure out a way to ambush him.

Patterning scrapes is anything but new. One of the earliest gurus of modern whitetail hunting, Bob McGuire, was also one of the first to try and determine where scrapes fit into a particular buck's overall pattern. Bob long ago counseled hunters on the fact that bucks would employ one of two major scrape patterns: linear scrapelines made by ridge-running bucks, and circular routes or "junkets" in agricultural areas.

One of McGuire's former employees, Alan Altizer of Blountville, Tennessee, has gone a step further. Altizer has gotten down to the nitty gritty by placing bucks into one of three categories, depending on what scrape pattern the animal follows. From that, and from close observation, he's been able to develop specific hunting strategies that work for each, and he's got the bucks to prove it, including the Tennessee state archery record typical.

"I was like everyone else," Altizer confided. "When I began hearing about scrapes, I'd pick one out to hunt, sit down, and give up days later because I hadn't seen anything. Then I began hunting river bottoms and ridgetops, and began to find a few scrapes where I could occasionally shoot something. Because of my limited success, I began taking a closer look at all scrapes.

"The most important thing I discovered was that scrape patterns are ruled by topography. Here in eastern Tennessee we have many different types of terrain. There are steep-sided mountains thousands of feet high, farm fields, woodlots, swamps, and thickets. I've found out through lots of field research that various bucks will use different scrape patterns depending on where and how they travel during the rut."

Altizer believes that there are three basic scraping patterns. Like McGuire, he also believes that some bucks run ridges and bottoms in a linear pattern while other bucks haunt agricultural areas with circular routes. But he's added yet another scrape pattern—one that he feels is the most productive of all—that of "cluster" scrapes.

"Take these bucks near my home," he explained.

"Where there's lots of agriculture, an animal's range may include many large fields with a few scattered woodlots where deer gather during the day. One buck that I know of in an area like this runs a 10-mile route in a circular pattern. It can take him 10 days to make an entire circuit."

Altizer knows of another buck that takes even longer to complete its 5-mile circular scrape route. "This buck will move into an area for a week or two and while he's there, really tear up the area scraping. But then he'll move out, often traveling a mile in one night to make it to the next woodlot. When he's traveling, this buck moves from woodlot to woodlot along fencerows. Hunting one of this buck's hot scrapes could work if he's still in the area and doesn't know you're around. But there's a far better chance that the buck will be long gone. If that's the case, you could spend many days hunting without seeing him at all."

Analyzing scrapes as critical parts of an animal's home range becomes imperative when bucks run large routes like these two animals did. To try to determine exactly what a buck is doing, Altizer first thoroughly scouts the area from the ground. Then, he inspects it again, this time using topographic maps and aerial photos, looking for travel lanes or geographic features that a wily buck deer will have to use when moving from place to place. He then marks every pertinent detail that he finds in an area on a topo map using a different symbol for items like scrapes, rubs, trails, beds, etc. Before long a definite pattern develops. "I'm always looking for spots like a crease or cut along a hill, a saddle across a ridgetop, or a spot where two or more ridges come together that may work like a funnel along a deer's route."

When someone is as single-minded as Altizer is about hunting trophy bucks, he'll come up with all types of tricks. "I found out that different bucks each have unique features and traits," he said. "One might prefer scraping on the sides of ridges, another will prefer scraping under a certain type of tree," he explained. "Some even make a particular shape of scrape. All this I note on my map. I'm often able to identify a particular buck by its rubs and tracks, especially if it's an older buck. And that's when tracking pits really come in handy."

Many of you are probably shaking your heads wondering what in the world tracking pits are. Eastern Tennessee, like many parts of the country, is crisscrossed with roads. Once Alan determines a buck's probable route, he begins to look for spots where the buck has to cross a road. When a buck travels a lengthy, circular junket, a set of tracks leading into a particular area, and no set leading out, is like finding an "At Home" sign posted on a tree. And tracking pits play a crucial role in his determination.

Whenever possible, Altizer looks for crossings where the roadsides are bare. He carries a rake in the back of his vehicle so he can rake out old tracks. That way, he can instantly spot new ones as he drives by, even from inside the car, and no one else knows what he's doing. He checks each tracking pit in an area before hunting each morning and again after he quits hunting in the evening. When a particular buck is holding tight in an area, Altizer won't quit hunting him until his tracks indicate that he's moved on.

"One interesting thing about hunting a buck like this is that if you've got some friends that you can trust, you can all hunt the same buck by carefully concentrating hunters in one area," he said. "Once I put my brother Mike in a place where I knew a buck was holding, and he got shots at not one but five different big bucks within a day and a half, bucks that would have scored between 110 and 160 Pope and Young points."

Sometimes a little finesse is called for. "When tracks tell me that a buck is holed up in a small woodlot, I'll have an alternate plan," he emphasized. "You just can't get up on a buck in a small area, so when this happens, I'll look for another area nearby where I might get a shot. For instance, once I found a crop-field that had lots of scrapes. Since does were using the area heavily as a food source, I knew they would help lure the buck out into the open. In this case, I hunted the field edge rather than the woodlot to keep from spooking the buck out of there completely."

If you do make some tracking pits, be careful, particularly if someone sees you with the rake; nasty rumors can get started. One landowner told Alan that he wouldn't be allowed to hunt on his farm anymore. When Alan asked why, the landowner told him that he knew what he was up to . . . he'd seen him out with his rake, and just knew he was planting pot back in the woods. Alan managed to clear his good name, but he's a lot more careful when he's using his rake these days.

But back to scrape patterns. Altizer says that bucks following circular patterns in his area generally move from one-half mile to one mile each day. But one buck he's been after for a couple of years will often move as much as four miles in a night. "I figure that when he moves that much, he's got a tail-wind so he can't rely on his nose," Alan said. "And there's not much cover along this route, either. He has to move a long way to get to an area where he can once again use his nose to warn him of danger."

Alan's methods are extremely effective because he really pays attention to every little detail; still, no foolproof legal method for hunting big whitetails has yet been devised. In this case, he hunted the particular buck hard for two long years, yet never managed to take him. "I had between three and ten different stands or blinds along one section he traveled," he explained. "And even though I saw him three or four times from as close as twenty yards, I never did get a clear shot."

After many years of paying meticulous attention to each type of scrape route, Alan has discovered that the bucks that run circular routes usually do so in a counterclockwise direction. "I don't know why, but that's what they do," he stated. "My guess is that it's also wind-related, probably something to do with the way the prevailing wind blows across an area."

Linear-scrape patterns are just that: a line of scrapes. Again, according to Altizer, these are also topography-oriented and usually occur along ridgetops in mountainous regions, along river or creek bottoms, or occasionally when five or six woodlots are strung out for a mile or two in an agricultural zone. Linear-scrape patterns are often quite short in actual distance covered. In fact, Altizer says it's not uncommon for bucks with linear routes to make all their scrapes along one ridgeline. Good spots to hunt a ridge-running buck include: (1) at a ridge intersection; (2) at a saddle; or, (3) at the scrape that shows the most use; but this means ferreting out every scrape along the route.

"Bucks with linear routes are often the easiest bucks to hunt," Altizer advised. "For one thing, if they're not pressured, these are the bucks that will be out and about all day. Even when they're bumped by someone else, since they hang out in heavily wooded areas they'll often feel secure enough to come back to their scrapeline later that same day."

Altizer has one example of a big ridge-running buck that survives to this day because of a tactic developed to deal with heavy hunting pressure. "When this deer would get bumped by hunters, he'd run off the ridge to a river," he said. "Then he'd swim across and onto the far shore. He'd follow the river for a while, cross back over again, then travel through a deep hollow until he could make his way back to his ridgetop. In one spot I found a dozen sets of this buck's tracks where he'd come out of the river, but no set of tracks going in, proving to me that this was a very definite escape route since I knew the buck ordinarily ran a linear line of scrapes."

Another good hunting technique for linear-pattern bucks is to set up several stands between scrapes, especially where natural bottlenecks occur. These will force bucks to come close enough to your stand position for a shot. If there are no spots like this, then concentrate on the hardest hit scrapes, setting up 30 or 40 yards downwind. Bucks often check their scrapes cautiously, from a distance. "Look for little pawed-out areas, beds, or what I call 'frustration' rubs," Altizer advised. "A buck scent-checking downwind sometimes butts his head against nearby brush. These areas are often found in real thick spots, or in a little dip in the topography. But when you find one, set up nearby."

Altizer says that still-hunting linear-scrape patterns is not only productive, it can be a lot of fun, too. "I'll stalk 30 to 50 yards off to one side of the line, yet keeping the buck's actual scrape route in sight," he explained. "Sometimes the topography won't be exactly right, so you may have to adjust the distance a little, but what you want to do is keep your eyes open as you move slowly from tree to tree. Every now and then, glass ahead. If you're lucky enough to see a buck, then try to work in front of him so that he comes to you. I've taken two different bucks like that."

Always keep the wind at your back when still-hunting linear scrapes, or else stalk into a crosswind since the buck should be ahead of you. Each technique can be extremely effective.

The final type of scrape pattern is also Altizer' s favorite: cluster scrapes. "You'll know it when you find a bunch of 'cluster' scrapes," Altizer said. "You can go into an area one day and find absolutely nothing. But two or three days later, there will be hundreds of scrapes in the same spot. Sometimes you can actually smell the scrapes; they'll stink similar to an elk wallow. As soon as you discover a place like this, set up at once, watch the wind, and stay there."

Cluster scrapes are often discovered during times of high hunting pressure. "The types of places where you'll find them are in what I call 'sanctuaries,' " Alan explained. "These are places within a buck's home range where he'll go to hide once hunters begin hassling him. I've found them in swamps, grown up clear-cuts, or almost any real thick area. But sanctuaries are usually very hard to hunt. Often they must be hunted from the ground because there's no good place to set up except on the ground. And don't forget, whenever you're hunting from the ground, pay attention to wind direction and thermals all day long. As soon as conditions change, switch your position."

Another Tennessee hunter, Luke Fuller of Kingsport, took the state's No. 1 non-typical whitetail (a monster with 30 points and a total Boone and Crockett score of 223) by hunting a scrape in a heavy thicket nine days after firearms season got underway. That same area continues to attract big deer. Two other non-typicals, one that scored 206 and another that scored 202, were taken within 200 yards of the same place where Luke

Fuller bagged his buck. Yet another trophy buck that scored 186 points as a non-typical at 2½ years of age was also taken there. One can only imagine what that deer would have scored when he was seven years old.

Altizer has found that cluster scrapes often crop up where the scrape routes of two mature bucks overlap. "I once located an area with 10 or 15 scrapes where the routes of two different bucks came together," Alan recalled. "Nearby was an area about 100 yards square that looked like it had been worked over by a rototiller, where it was plain that the two bucks had fought. My friend and I managed to take both of these bucks with a bow. The week before we did, they'd both had really good racks. But by the time we shot them, their racks were all broken up. My friend's buck still had nine points, but he was missing one point entirely, a big hunk off his main beam, and had broken off one of his brow tines. Even with 22 or 23 inches of deductions, the rack scored 139 Pope and Young points."

Altizer feels any scrape that's been urinated in recently is an ideal area from which to call and rattle. "I've rattled in nine or ten bucks to the bow from around fresh scrapes," he confided, "even though I was only able to take three of them. Calling and rattling when you're bowhunting by yourself on the ground can be pretty tricky. When calling or rattling like this, I get my best results when I'm set up right over the scrape. Often a big buck will be bedded within 50 or 100 yards of his fresh scrape, and will charge right in. Bucks can be real protective of their scrapes when they think they're being challenged by another buck."

While understanding scrape patterns is important to deciphering the ways of whitetails, these same scrape patterns are by no means consistent over the deer's entire range, which covers a tremendous amount of ground from Central America to Canada. The patterns explained here are probably applicable over much of North America, yet there are notable exceptions, especially in areas where deer migrate during their rutting seasons.

"I agree pretty much with what Alan says about scrape patterns, at least in the eastern U.S.," said Billy Goebel, who used to live in Seeley Lake, Montana, but has recently returned to Tennessee. "But it's a whole different ballgame in western Montana. Scrape activity there ranges from slim to none, even in areas with an unbelievable amount of whitetail activity."

If you're one of those hunters who has written off scrapes as a lost cause, perhaps it's time to reconsider. Scrape pattern know-how for your neck of the whitetail woods could mean the difference between success and failure from now on!

17

Sold on Swamps

By Kathy Etling
(October 1994)

The researcher was puzzled. He had his radio-transmitter turned on and its signal was loud and clear. The buck had to be here somewhere—somewhere close—but for the life of him, the biologist didn't know where it could be. The man took another step. The green swamp water undulated softly around his body, making large circles that gently sloshed away, until they finally broke upon the grass tussocks and small earth ridges that jutted above the swampy water. Birds swooped and darted above him, but still he couldn't find the deer. The man looked intensely at each tussock, dissecting every bit of dry ground he could see. He knew how tightly whitetails would hold to cover when humans closed in on them. It was obvious this buck was doing exactly that.

Suddenly, the water in front of him boiled. A small buck splashed up straight out of the swamp mud, less than three feet from where the researcher stood. The man was too surprised to react for a moment, but then be realized how effectively this buck had adapted a woodland whitetail's

Big bucks prefer to stay in the safe haven of swamps even in cold weather.
Credit: Bob Etling

evasion tactics for its own swampy use. The animal had remained completely still, standing quietly in water that covered everything but its nostrils, eyes, and the top of its head, as the biologist came closer and closer. Finally, when the man got too close to tolerate, even for a survivor like this deer, the animal burst from its soggy hiding place and splashed away . . . alternately swimming and running until out of sight.

The researcher was noted whitetail biologist Dr. Larry Marchinton of the University of Georgia's School of Forest Resources. Larry is a swamp hunter in his own right, so he could appreciate how well this young buck had hidden from him.

"Whitetails will do anything to avoid humans," he explained. "Older bucks are particularly adept at escaping hunters. And that means local deer soon learn how they can use swamps to get away from people.

"Deer move into swamps for other reasons, too," he continued. "If they're being bothered by deer flies or mosquitoes, they'll go into the swamp and submerge themselves to avoid getting bit."

The southern portion of the U.S. is loaded with swamps. And while some hunters take full advantage of the opportunities that wetland bogs and swamps present, others avoid them like the proverbial plague. Yet swamps can provide some of the country's best hunting—whether they're the bogs or cedar swamps of the northern reaches, the upper Midwest's pothole country, the sloughs and marshes of the lower Midwest, or the cypress/tupelo gum swamps of the Deep South.

The Deep South in particular is noted for the immensity of its swampy regions. From South Carolina's low country to marshes near the Florida Everglades, to the Mississippi Delta, southern whitetails both live and thrive in swamps. And those hunters who learn to adapt to the swamps (like the whitetails they hunt) soon realize this kind of hunting can be incredibly productive. Some hunt the swamps just like they hunt the uplands; by utilizing whitetail sign and then placing treestands accordingly. Others devise techniques especially suited for swamp hunting. Still others resort to slip-hunting, a term that many of us equate with still-hunting, while others may think of it as stalking. No matter what you call it or how you do it, hunting whitetails in southern swamps is one of the best ways ever to bag your deer.

Take Billy Macoy for example. Billy, a well-known whitetail hunter from Lineville, Alabama, hunts and guides on lands owned and leased by Southern Sportsman Hunting Lodge (5977 Highway 17, Hayneville, AL 36040). I was lucky enough to hunt the swamps with Billy, and know the amount of time and effort he puts into assessing whitetail sign and movement patterns around these swamps.

"The last couple of seasons, the swamps have been drier than usual," Billy said. "And hunters must learn to reckon with that. As strange as it may sound, we hunt waterholes inside the swamps, potholes or spring seepages that provide water early in the season, but are covered with water once fall and winter rains arrive."

Billy scouts for sign early in the season and continues scouting until the peak of the rut in mid-January. "You'll find scrapes on high ground," he explained. "Swamps are like any other topography. You'll have high spots—ridges; and low spots—the valleys. The valleys fill with water when the rains come. The ridges stay exposed and that's where bucks scrape.

"Bucks also rub on oaks and alders," he continued. "They'll even wade out into the water to rub on trees. Find a place full of buck sign and hunt it the same way you'd hunt anywhere else. Be sure you place several different stands in an area to take advantage of the wind."

Billy is especially keen on thick draws full of deer sign. He feels the largest bucks avoid the open woods when they can stick to heavier cover. He places his stand so he can see under nearby vegetation. If a stand is too high, you'll have trouble seeing through the greenery and down to the ground.

"You'll always hear swamp deer before you see them," he explained. "Early in the season, you'll hear them moving through the palmettos. You don't actually hear the palmettos hitting against the deer; you'll hear the palmetto leaves slapping against each other once the deer's passed through them. Later, after the rains have started, you'll hear deer splashing through the water." Like most southern swamp hunters, Billy Macoy relies on food sources, too. "Our swamps have all kinds of acorns," he said. "Some acorns start falling in September. Others fall well into January. And early in the season, we hunt areas full of honeysuckle and green browse."

Billy believes swamps produce best during the early morning and late afternoon. Yet if he finds a place that hasn't been disturbed by other hunters, he'll hunt it in midday, too. Billy's tactics produce. He guided a 16-year-old client to a giant swamp buck that field-dressed 280 pounds. Billy harvested a great swamp buck that scored 150 Boone and Crockett points.

David Lyons, one of the owners of Southern Sportsman, is another hunter who's sold on swamps. David is partial to swamp scrape hunting, and he's taken an 8-point buck with a 20-inch inside spread using this method.

"You must set your stand well off the scrapeline," he advised, "yet keep it in a place where you can still see the scrape. Normally, swamp deer won't come right to their scrapes. They'll stay about 50 or 75 yards downwind. That's where you want to be."

David thinks swamp hunting is much better during the morning hours. "It seems to me as though larger bucks will only leave the swamps after dark," he mused. "I think they go out to feed in nearby fields and to size up the does. When the does dawdle back to the swamp late the next morning, it's a good time to pick off one of the bucks following them."

Bobby Gates is a private landowner in the Hayneville area. He's a good friend (I met him while hunting at Southern Sportsman) and a successful hunter who has taken many good whitetails from nearby swamps.

"I like to cut deer off as they make their way from bedding to feeding areas," Bobby said. "Deer love to bed in brushy thickets or dense canebrakes. I know how much because a timber company recently clear-cut a four-acre plot near my home. I soon discovered the bucks really started using it as a bedding area. It's full of honeysuckle and small woody stems where deer can hide and feel safe.

"Another tactic that works, if you have access to some land, is to plant plots of improved white clover next to swamps. Deer love the stuff. When they leave the swamp to feed on it, you can often get a shot." Bobby hunts from treestands, but he says it's hard to stay on stand after 8 a.m. "I almost have to get out to see what's going on," he admitted.

One tactic of which he's fond is to stalk with the wind in his favor, either blowing in his face or quartering towards him. "This is a good technique for January when bucks are moving all day," he explained. "It really doesn't matter what time of day you hunt. The bucks will be nosing around, just like bird dogs, from morning to night. I bagged a really nice 8-point this year when stalking. He was following a ridge trail through the swamp, heading back to his bedding area. I watched him coming for quite a while before I could see what size rack he had. He just kept coming and I began using my grunt call, trying to get his attention and make him stop. Finally, he heard me. He stopped and I was able to shoot between two trees. He ran 50 yards and piled up."

Bobby says it's more important to be certain of your shots when hunting swamps than when hunting uplands or forests. "You'll lose a poor blood trail even faster in a swamp full of water," he said.

Phil Riddle, a taxidermist from Alexander City, Alabama, bow-hunts the swamps. "I have my best luck in the morning, from 8 to 11," he said. "I also really concentrate on food sources, things like chestnut oak acorns or white oak acorns early, persimmons a little later on. Persimmons are really good, if you can find them. Deer also like the pods from black locust trees. They have a sweet taste deer seem to crave."

Later Phil hunts the does. He will set his stand up on main trails. Those leading from swamps into nearby soybean fields are good. So are trails leading to late-bearing mast trees such as red oaks.

The Alabama swamps near Hayneville are but one example of southern wetlands. Dave Moreland, a deer-study leader with the Louisiana Department of Wildlife and Fisheries in Baton Rouge, hunts a different kind of swamp. "Here in Louisiana, many of the hunters hunt cypress/tupelo habitat in pirogues (pronounced *peeroes*). A pirogue is a traditional Cajun boat. It's made of wood and looks something like a canoe. In pure swamp areas, like Louisiana's 16,000-acre Joyce Wildlife Management Area in the lower portion of Tangipahoa Parish, hunters have to use pirogues. It's the only way to get around."

Dave says there are two effective ways to hunt cypress/tupelo habitats. "Get a map and locate the scattered hardwood ridges," he said. "Then find a way in, either in a pirogue or by wearing waders and walking in. You can either hunt with a gun out of the pirogue, or stalk along as you ease through the water on foot. Lots of hunters combine a swamp deer hunt with an early morning duck hunt. It's a good way to do both."

Dave Moreland says that because Louisiana's swampland habitat is so tough and difficult to hunt, you'll find a good age-class structure of bucks in the swamps. Interestingly enough, he says that the hooves of swamp deer grow longer to give them better footing in mud and water. Moreland says to look for rubs on small cypress trees, particularly those growing along spoil banks. Spoil banks—the mud and dirt that's been dredged from canals and river channels to expedite barge traffic and then piled on the sides of these waterways—are major deer travel corridors.

"Deer are remarkable," Dave said. "When there's a lot of hunting pressure, they'll just go out and stand in the water. I use hip boots to cross sloughs and work my way out to the slight ridges running through the swamps. You don't have to go too far to get away either. But always take a compass and a map with you. On cloudy days or if you're not familiar with the area, you can get totally turned around without them."

Some important whitetail mast species to seek out in the cypress/tupelo gum swamps are the swamp cow oaks, water oaks, and overcup oaks. Deer also feed freely on all sorts of herbaceous plants and forbs that grow in swamps. One favorite is alligator weed.

Dave feels that the Mississippi River Delta country is another important wetland habitat of which whitetail hunters should be aware. "Whenever the river comes up, there's a lot of backwater flooding in nearby wildlife management areas," he said. "That forces deer onto spoil bank levees. It concentrates them and makes it easier for hunters to take good bucks." Acorns from nuttall oaks are prime whitetail forage in Mississippi Delta country.

As for public land, Louisiana operates a number of swamp areas that are made to order for whitetail hunters. The Pearl River Management Area features 32,000 swampy acres in St. Tammany Parish near Slidell. Look for deer feeding on acorns from the obetusa oak, a cross between the water oak and laurel oak.

Also, there are two wildlife areas in the famous Atchafalaya Basin. The 40,000-acre Sherburne WMA and the 25,000-acre Attakapas WMA can only be accessed by boat, yet offer superb deer hunting

"When Hurricane Andrew hit the Atchafalaya Basin [ten] years ago, it knocked down a lot of timber," Dave Moreland explained. "That opened up the canopy, creating browse and cover. Not only is the deer herd increasing in number, their physical condition is improving."

Moreland says people also hunt deer successfully in coastal marshes. Again the key to success is to concentrate on ridges, either natural ones or man-made spoil banks created during oil and gas exploration. "Most hunters work the marshes from tripod stands since they can see a long way," he explained. "Others use dogs."

One last swamp master is Joe Hamilton, founder of the Quality Deer Management Association (P.O. Box 8116, Greenwood, SC 29649; 803-229-5502) and a wildlife biologist who studied under Dr. Larry Marchinton.

"I hunt South Carolina's low country," Joe said. "The kind of swamps I hunt lie close to major rivers. Because these areas flood regularly, especially in winter, you get a ridge and a valley system. Nearby rice fields will also hold deer. Cattails provide them with enough cover so that they do very well.

"The prime activity times for deer in any of these areas is early morning and late afternoon. But when the rut is in full swing, I'll stay out all day long.

"I've found that the best way to hunt these swamps is stalking or slip-hunting," Joe continued. "My favorite time to stalk is during damp weather, even in a drizzling rain, because you can move so quietly. In my opinion, if you hunt during wet weather, you must stick to neck shots. You'll either miss, make a fatal shot, or flesh wound the animal.

"Never shoot offhand at a swamp deer. That's the surest way to wound it. And if you wound one, you'll have a hard time recovering it because of all the water. Use a shooting stick, that's a great help. Or lean against a tree, take time to get a good rest, or simply don't shoot at all.

"Always stalk directly into the wind, or quarter into it," Hamilton advised. "Wear light boots. You may get wet, but I never worry much about it until it's coming in my shirt pockets.

"Play the sunlight, too," he said. "Keep it at your back so it confuses the deer's sense of sight.

"If you're stalking through dry areas where you might make a lot of noise, don't worry about it," Hamilton explained. "Just worry about how you're making it. Anyone who spends much time around deer, turkeys, or squirrels knows they move a short distance and then stop, move a short distance and stop. Move just like they do, in spurts. When you stop, do so in a shadow to avoid glare from your gun or clothing. Don't sneak. I really think animals get more upset by a little noise than by a lot of noise. Think about it. Predators couldn't operate if they made a lot of noise. How many noisy bobcats have you heard? Anything that's making a lot of noise won't startle animals nearly as much as a sneaky noise.

"Take a diaphragm with you and yelp yourself through the woods."

Hamilton also said that any time two habitat types bump up together, creating an edge, it's a prime place for hunters to set their stands.

"Hunting along the edge of a swamp is a great technique," he stated. "Try to find where, and when, whitetails are leaving swamps, and then try to catch them in transit."

Hamilton listed the tremendous variety of mast available in the low country, everything from willow oak, laurel oak, water oak, cherry bark oak, southern red oak, overcup oak, and the ever popular swamp chestnut oak.

One last hint? "People scouting for deer spend too much time looking down at the ground and not enough time looking up," Hamilton concluded. "Swamp hunters should pay attention to details like scrapes and rubs and trails. But they should take binoculars along early in the season to learn which trees will have good acorn crops. That's the best natural food plot you can have." And it's free.

Some of our country's most impressive deer call southern swamps home. Hunt one soon. Like me, you may be sold on swamps forever.

Before you go . . .

Always be certain of the laws in the state or county in which you're swamp hunting. A few states (Missouri is one) have laws against shooting deer while they're in the water. Other states make it illegal to shoot a deer from a motorized boat. In some, you can't shoot from any boat, even an unmotorized one. And along South Carolina's Cape Fair River and its tributaries, it's even illegal to have a high-powered rifle or a shotgun with buckshot in your boat during deer season.

The author four-wheels it out of a swamp with a trophy buck.
Credit: Bob Etling

18

The Art and Science of Preparing Venison

by Dave Henderson
(Spring 1996)

As a young man, I ate anything, and plenty of it. A cast iron stomach and a set of decidedly indifferent taste buds were the saviors of our early marriage.

In those days, "delicious" and "edible" were code names we applied to food. If something was "delicious," it meant we were at someone else's house and seconds were in order. If a meal was "edible," it meant we were home and hadn't gone face-first in the plate after the first bite.

I don't want to say that my wife couldn't cook, but we were the only couple I ever knew of who prayed *after* our meals. She used the hallway smoke detector as an oven timer. Her meat loaf glowed in the dark.

The author's family relies totally on venison for its red meat year-round.
Credit: Dave Henderson

But despite my remarkably adaptive and forgiving traits, we did reach occasional contretemps over food. For instance, if a piece of meat looked anything like it was part of an animal, bird, or fish, Debbie didn't want any part of it. No hair, veins, blood, pin feathers, etc.

Thus, when those first cuts of personally butchered venison arrived in our tiny apartment, a standoff ensued. After a horrific scream, she explained in graphic and very definite terms what I could do with the bloody tissue, and how the supermarket was the only suitable source of trimmed (disguised) and cleaned meat.

Fortunately, the cooler head prevailed that day. As the man of the house, I explained that since I had a crummy, low-paying job, and she didn't even have one, our grocery budget was extremely limited. I explained that we were little more than modern hunter-gatherers, and what I hunted and gathered would have to go a long way toward feeding us.

I also introduced her to my collection of deer and venison books that day. My authoritative demeanor—and an on-my-knees promise to trim, clean, and wrap venison more appropriately—apparently struck a chord.

It wasn't an overnight transformation, but it was a dramatic one. Today the former Ms. Debra Pickering makes a breaded venison tenderloin that would make the ghost of Escoffier writhe with envy. Rolled neck roasts, marinated steaks and butterfly chops, venison parmesan, venison meatballs, venison piccatta, venison diane, and an assortment of ground venison casseroles and dishes are staples in our household, and are eagerly anticipated by both of us. She has, in fact, co-authored the book *Venison: A Users' Manual for Deer Hunters* with me.

We study venison cookbooks like textbooks, and have a large collection, the Bible of which, by the way, is fellow Buckmasters columnist John Weiss's 1984 classic, *Venison: From Field to Table.*

We are, today, true venison lovers, and gain no pleasure in trying to "trick" an avowed anti-venison person into eating a well-prepared (some call it disguised) piece of deer meat. Heck, no. If they don't want it, let's not waste it; it's their loss. We haven't bought beef in more than ten years, venison and elk meat filling our red meat budget.

When our daughter was a preschooler, she one day referred to hamburger served at my in-laws' as a "deerburger." When my mother-in-law explained that this burger was made from beef rather than venison, the flabbergasted four-year-old said with incredulous disgust: "You mean, you eat COWS?"

Combating "Gamey" Taste

Depending as heavily on venison as we do means that we must use a variety of tactics to neutralize the various factors that might give our deer meat a "gamey" taste. I'm not talking about the distinctive flavor imparted by what the animal ate. Venison from a Pennsylvania deer that lived in a laurel patch will differ appreciably in taste from that of an Alabama deer that dined regularly on honeysuckle, or an Oklahoma whitetail from sage country, or an alfalfa and corn-fed deer from farm country.

No, the taste we seek to neutralize comes from the meat's condition, how long it was aged, how it was dressed, handled, and transported, and its state at the time it was killed.

Knowing and dealing with these conditions can mean the difference between delightful table fare and something resembling Fido's bedding.

For instance, if the meat was aged too long or improperly—we're not talking spoiled, but rather strong-smelling—you can bet it's going to have that infamous "gamey" taste. If the animal was highly stressed before death, either by a poorly placed shot or a hard run, the meat is apt to be dark and sticky. It's depleted, not acidic like the muscles of a relaxed animal, and thus more prone to early spoilage.

Many venison experts advise coating the meat of a stressed animal in vinegar; adding the missing acidity. Others say marinate it in olive oil or Italian dressing.

You may also find that the meat of an older buck, particularly one that has been rutting, will be tougher and have a stronger taste. We treat this meat the same way we do that of a stressed deer. Soak the meat in milk for four to six hours in the refrigerator. This can be done after the meat is thawed or while it's thawing.

The meat of a stressed deer, by the way, should not be aged. Get the hide off, cut it up, and freeze it as soon as possible. Because of the lack of acidity, it provides an excellent medium for bacterial growth; hence, the strong smell and/or propensity to spoil quickly.

All blood-shot portions should be removed entirely and the surrounding meat soaked in salt water in the refrigerator for a couple of hours to draw out the blood in the tissue. Be sure to always trim all fat and the silver film that clothes large muscle groups.

Proper butchering and preparation can make delectable table fare of any cut of meat from any deer, regardless of shot placement, the animal's age or sex, how far it ran, or curing time. If you can't cut across the grain of the meat, one of the great equalizers is to slice the cut very thin— a half-inch isn't too thin—and pound it with a tenderizing mallet or butcher knife. Break down the fibers and you'll be able to cut it with a fork without using any additives.

Why Hang a Carcass?

Some meat experts claim that since deer meat does not have fat marbled through it like beef, there is no advantage to hanging the carcass. This group suggests getting the hide off the animal immediately to release body heat as quickly as possible, then cutting, wrapping, and freezing the meat the same day. This meat can be aged somewhat by defrosting it in a refrigerator for a couple of days.

Others suggest that you age the meat to break down muscle fiber and thus tenderize the meat before butchering. The latter philosophy is the most widely practiced. There is, by the way, a right way to age a carcass. Ideally, the skinned carcass should be hung, neck down, in controlled temperatures of 34-36 degrees in 40 to 50 percent humidity for several days. That's ideal for tenderizing the meat and keeping moisture in it. But how many of us have those controlled conditions in our garage, shed, or front yard maple tree?

It's obviously better to leave it to a professional who has a meat cooler. I shy away from those processors who cut meat with a bandsaw—spreading the bone marrow and sinew. Have the meat boned, take out the back loin, and cut it into butterfly chops rather than having it sawed pork-chop style. Then have it double-wrapped, airtight, for freezer storage.

Venison Tips

Here are some things to keep in mind when dealing with venison:

- Marinating venison is a good means of changing or disguising its taste, and sometimes of tenderizing the meat. But marinating does rob the meat of some of its nutrients.
- High heat can quickly dry out and toughen a cut of venison. Cook slowly and sparingly. Wild game meat has no fat. Use fat or oil to provide moisture while cooking.
- Although venison is touted as a health food, some cuts actually have more cholesterol than beef.
- Ground venison is usually prepared with beef suet or pork fat mixed in to provide moisture and fat. A 6- or 7-to-1 mix contains just enough fat to provide moisture while cooking, but will be melted by the time the meat is done.
- Any organs considered for table fare—heart, liver, kidneys—should be soaked in salt water for a couple of hours to draw out the blood. Organ meat is best eaten the same day the animal is killed. It can be frozen but loses some of its taste.
- Properly wrapped (double-wrapped in freezer paper, airtight) can be stored in a freezer for more than a year without a loss of flavor or texture.
- Thawed venison in a transparent wrap should only be stored in the refrigerator for up to two days. Meat wrapped in brown paper may be re-

frigerated three to five days, but should be unwrapped, placed on a platter or tray, and loosely covered.

Is Venison Heart-Healthy?

Whether or not something is good or bad for you apparently depends on who has had research money lately.

Coffee is a good example. Various studies in recent years have proven conclusively that decaffeinated coffee is either 1) much better or 2) much worse for you than coffee with caffeine. The use of vitamin supplements is another area where one says something, the other the opposite, and both have scientific proof.

Well, the controversy has spread into the field of venison.

In 1988, North Dakota State and the University of Wyoming published studies that trashed the conventional thinking of venison as a health food.

The North Dakota study showed that the cholesterol content of hunter-killed venison was more than half again as high as beef (116.3 mg per gram of venison compared to 70.9 mg per gram of beef). The Wyoming study showed that mule deer meat taken during the hunting season had a 10 percent higher cholesterol content than beef.

The news shook a lot of people, especially those whose doctors had advised venison as the staple of a low-cholesterol diet.

Think about it. You've probably never heard from or read a reputable source that touted the low cholesterol levels in venison. Most people, you see, confuse fat with cholesterol, and venison is indeed very low in fat.

Since venison, beef, and pork all vary in their fat and cholesterol levels, deer hunters frequently ask how these meats compare in their potential effect on the serum cholesterol level, one of the risk factors in cardiovascular disease.

Doctors tell us that the medical recommendations to reduce serum cholesterol by diet include such factors as 1) reduction in total calories; 2) reduction in total fat; 3) reduction in saturated fat; and 4) reduction in dietary cholesterol.

Not only is venison lower in calories than beef, but boneless venison from does contains fewer calories per 100 grams than meat from bucks. Venison and beef have about the same levels of saturated fatty acids. Venison, however, remains lower in monounsaturated fatty acids and higher in polyunsaturated fatty acids.

The North Dakota State University study found that venison loin contains slightly more phosphorous, magnesium, iron, copper, and manganese than beef loin, but lesser amounts of potassium, sodium, calcium, and zinc.

Typically, several more recent studies have contradicted the North Dakota findings and seemingly reaffirmed venison's value. A recent magazine article noted that new studies conclude that a three-ounce cut of venison leg is lower in fat (5 gm), cholesterol (62 gm), and calories (139), than beef (13 gm of fat, 77 cholesterol, 223 calories), lamb (8, 80, 183), veal (4, 112, 155), and pork (13, 80, 219).

Not only that, the studies show venison to have less cholesterol than chicken (72 mg) and it falls far below the American Heart Association's guidelines for calories, fat, and cholesterol.

These studies were done by the U.S. Department of Agriculture, ESHA Research, and the National Food Laboratory, Inc. Researchers at Texas A&M University reached similar conclusions in regard to comparing calories and fat in venison, beef, and chicken.

In addition, scientists at the Texas Department of Agriculture also compared venison with chicken in caloric and cholesterol content, and reached the same results.

Regardless of the conclusions, all agree that venison is still a very healthy red meat. That's why doctors recommend it. Not only is it extremely low in fat, as we said, but venison from a white-tailed deer contains a unique balance of protein, fats, and minerals (plus a full complement of essential amino acids) that provide man with a very complete food item of very high biological value in a very concentrated form.

Dr. Ken Drew of New Zealand noted the studies during a lecture at the 1990 International Biology of Deer Symposium at Mississippi State University.

"If science had been commissioned to produce 'designer' red meat that had all the best attributes of our traditional farm animals and none of the perceived bad features, the remarkable result would have been something remarkably like venison," Drew said. Remember, too, that he was addressing an audience of deer growers.

Marinating can add a different flavor to venison, and helps to tenderize it.
Credit: Dave Henderson

There probably is a very simple reason for the difference in the findings of the two studies. Cholesterol content, it turns out, varies with several factors. The species, the specific muscle, the sampling procedure, the type of feed the animal lived on, and whether or not the meat was cooked, all have a bearing on the cholesterol count.

The differences in the studies, it was felt, probably resulted from feed sources and the ages of the animals. The beef samples used in the North Dakota study came from animals fed a commercial fattening ration and slaughtered at 18 months. The deer samples were from older wild animals, and obviously, there was no control over the deer's food sources.

The U.S. Department of Agriculture, in an April 1989 handbook, listed cholesterol value of raw deer meat between 45 and 145 gm. The mean value thus is 85 gm, which approximates the other studies' findings.

So there, we're fine. At least until another study comes out.

19

The Tools of Time

By Tim Wells
(October 1996)

Through the mist of an evening fog came the dainty gender of the white-tail species, a young doe. As she strode below my stand, the distinctive grunt of a buck emerged from her back-trail. Slowly, I shifted my attention to the direction of the muffled sounds. Intently, I scanned the dense under-brush for a mere glimpse of the buck about to make his debut. I waited. Time slowly passed.

At last, I saw him. From the shadows of fading light he slid into view. His blocky frame rippled with mass, and his rack weighed heavy with tines and width. Preoccupied with his lust, the mature whitetail fol-lowed the doe toward my hide. I eased the bow into position as the buck closed the distance between us. It had taken months of strategic planning, not to mention countless hours and days of hunting without sight or sound of what now stood before me. I had paid my dues with time. As the knock touched the corner of my cheek, the reward was finally within grasp.

The author with a magnificent trophy. Proper timing of your hunt is critical. *Credit: Tim Wells*

Time can be a bowhunter's greatest ally or his worst adversary. The amount of time available to dedicate to hunting highly influences the success rate of the whitetail hunter. Success on big whitetails must be of interest to you, or you wouldn't be peddling through these pages of *Buckmasters*. Thus, it's important to recognize that one of the main elements in bowhunting trophy-class deer is time. The restrictions that govern our time are often beyond our control: Work, family life, and other responsibilities can greatly hamper the outcome of a whitetail season. If you've set your sites on shooting a trophy-class whitetail, consider a couple of suggestions that may aid you in your time-demanding quest: Quit your job, disconnect your phone, and divorce your spouse! That should clear the way for plenty of time afield. Although there is always the possibility that you'll lose your bow in the court proceedings, in which case you may want to reconsider the whole idea.

Seriously, if your time is limited, then it's imperative that you should use that time wisely if you're wanting to bag a record-class buck.

Most successful trophy hunters will admit that if they only had one week a year to hunt, they'd probably reconsider trophy whitetail hunting with a bow. It's all relative. Those who spend the most time afield, and also use that time wisely, will obviously have greater odds of success—although there are hunters who hunt every day of the season but have yet to bag Mr. Big. Many are not concerned with taking a big whitetail. Others may have failed to look closely at their approach to a very intricate game of cat and mouse.

If your time is limited (as it is with most hunters), then evaluate your current whitetail policies and the history of success you've had by using them. If you're not seeing big bucks, then I'd say that's your first clue to try a new approach. I've come to realize that even though I'm lucky enough to spend more time in the woods than the average hunter, I still have to strategically use my time according to the things that influence it. Otherwise, my success in seeing mature bucks will be greatly hampered.

Various situations occur each year that we as hunters have little control over: weather, moon phases, rut, leaf drop, competition from other hunters, natural death of a target animal, and numerous other variables may occur, causing good or bad effects on our overall success. For those who are not prepared to react to the changes that await their season's hunt, the inevitable generally occurs!

Weather, unlike moon phases or the rut, is not a variable that can be accurately predicted—at least not weeks in advance. Unfortunately, many of us have to schedule vacations weeks or even months in advance; thus, we often end up hunting in driving rains or boiling heat. Although I could discuss weather and its effects on deer movement for a hundred more pages, it's probably only necessary to briefly review the general rules of how weather affects deer movements, and the impact it may have on the hunter's time afield.

If your time is limited and you intend to hunt from a stationary position such as a treestand, it's imperative to know how the weather will affect deer movement, because waiting is the name of the game. If you have the luxury of scheduling a day off within a relatively short period of time, keep a close eye on the weather forecast.

The timing of your hunt can mean the difference between success and failure to see a big whitetail. Knowing what weather systems are favorable for hunting is a step toward the adrenaline stage. Warm weather is definitely a time to go to work. If 30 degrees is the norm for the time of year you're considering to hunt, and the predicted weather pattern is to range in the mid 50s, it's probably a good idea to wait for the weather to change toward cooler conditions, then use that valuable vacation time.

Big bucks drastically drop off daily travel activity during unseasonably warm weather. Bow season, which generally falls around the first of October, is a period when deer are putting on their winter coats and, prior to rut, have built up fat supplies. Warm temperatures leave them uncomfortable and lackadaisical. Even rut can be a slow period if unseasonably warm weather persist.

Hunters often ask me when the rut is to kick in so that they can schedule their hunting time to coincide with deer movements. That can be a tough question to answer when you consider the effects weather may have. The daily amount of light that enters a deer's eye is considered by most experts as the element that triggers the rut. Thus, I could almost predict the exact days that the rut will kick in, but that doesn't always ensure heavy buck activity will coincide. Weather conditions heavily impact the intensity of the rut. This doesn't mean that deer aren't breeding during warm weather; instead, they may not be courting with the full gusto evident during cooler weather.

A buck that picks up a twenty-minute-old track of a doe in heat on a hot muggy day probably won't be as aroused as he would on a cool, clear day. Bucks will often wait for evening and the cooler temperatures that accompany darkness. Warm temperatures that persist throughout a rut can spell lower buck harvest rates than rut periods accompanied by cool weather. Windy days also cause bucks to hold tight. It cuts down the acute ability their senses have in forewarning them of danger. If you have the opportunity to schedule your hunting time at will, avoid hot weather. The implications are simple if you're a stand hunter: cool, calm days make good sick days, unless your boss hunts the same neck of the woods you do.

Stationary hunters should also evaluate other variables besides weather that will influence the effectiveness of their time waiting on a stand. Hunting pressure is one of many reasons most quality bucks maintain a nocturnal advantage over hunters. Evaluate how much pressure exists in the area you're hunting. If you feel that it's extreme enough to cause the smartest whitetails to go 100 percent nocturnal, then what good does hunting from a stationary position do you? The gamble you're taking is that other hunters will hopefully bump into Mr. Big, or possibly there will be an eclipse of the sun and the bucks will be fooled into thinking it's dark and safe. Both are pretty much long shots, especially for bowhunters. Sometimes the dilemma can be resolved by merely going mobile, better known as still-hunting.

Ninety percent of big whitetails are taken by hunters who are hunting from treestands or ground blinds, but that doesn't mean that hunting from a stationary position is the most effective way to utilize your hunting time. Instead, other methods of hunting should be considered when stand hunting conditions are not favorable. Most hunters who consistently take big bucks with a bow have a host of tricks up their sleeves on how to fool big whitetails. Still-hunting, stand hunting, driving deer, and the various methods of calling and ambushing rutting deer should all be considered to prevent wasted time. If you're only prepared to use one method of hunting, your long-term success will reflect your shortcomings. If you're caught up in the middle of your season's hunt and the method you're using is turning up no signs of big bucks, being patient is not the answer—unless you're happy with one, or maybe two, good bucks a lifetime. Trophy hunters must be innovative if they want to trick the slickest animal on the continent.

Each year I set plans on how to wisely use my time hunting. I try to correlate my activities to that of my quarry. If the bucks are on the move, I'll be sitting on the stand. If bucks are not moving, I will be. Knowing the likelihood of how much a buck will be on the go has an obvious impact on how much moving around I do, if any at all. By going mobile when deer are not, and sitting when deer are on the move, you'll enhance your hunting time considerably.

In early season, I become mobile, still-hunting thickets and other buck lairs. This is a period when deer are lazy, hot, and rarely on the move. Yet on occasion, if a cold snap hits, I'll sit near a bedding area in hopes of catching a buck en route to food at last light.

As pre-rut approaches, bucks begin to move around in search of an early comer to estrus. In response, I continue to still-hunt, but I also incorporate grunt calling, rattling, and longer moments of stationary observations into my still-hunt. Once the rut begins, I climb into my stand for the duration. Furthermore, as long as the weather patterns hold cool or at least close to normal temperatures, I remain stationary. Rut is obviously an ideal time to sit if the deer are not under unusual circumstances, such as heat or extreme hunting pressure. And of course, there is a substantial amount of time involved in planning where I place my stand or ground blinds.

Post-rut, I once again go into a moderately slow still-hunt again, incorporating calling into my hunt. By the close of the season, I return to the trees near centralized areas where deer are feeding. Extreme cold snaps during late season seem to pull bucks to food sources even during legal hunting light. That's probably due to the fact that less hunters are in the woods, and the deer's hunger is greater than ever before in the season.

It doesn't matter how many hours you spend in the timber, or what the weather, moon, or other hunters are doing while you're there. Unless there's a mature buck in the area you're hunting, you'll be back to the main problem you set out to overcome. Wasted Time. Big whitetails are fewer in number than most hunters believe. Less than 1 percent of all bowhunters will harvest a book buck this fall! Thus, by not locating a good buck prior to season, you're likely to end up in the 99 percent category.

Each season, I try to have, at the very least, two good bucks located. Visual contact is obviously the best way to verify the general location of a good buck, but sometimes I'll even settle for a set of sheds or exceptional tracks that I've found prior to season. I look for anything that could be a good indicator that I'm in a buck's whereabouts. Up until two days prior to my '94 season, I had made plans to hunt a record-class 10-pointer that I'd seen feeding in an alfalfa field earlier that summer. Then one morning as I rounded a bend in the road near the buck's home turf, I realized I'd never get the opportunity to hunt the buck, for he was laying with his legs in an upright position along the road. Seems he'd met a bumper bullet sometime in the night. It was a sad case, but would have been doubly sad if I hadn't located other bucks prior to season. Pinpointing as many target animals as possible prior to opening day will keep you from scrambling around during season, ultimately wasting your valuable hunting time.

Additionally, I'm constantly trying to obtain access to new areas that hold good buck habitat. It's better to have more places to hunt than you have time for, than not enough places to hunt for all your time. Occasionally, I'll lose a good hunting area due to a change of ownership or additional hunting pressure. That's always discouraging, but even more discouraging is not having an alternative place to hunt. Good hunting time could once again be wasted.

Time is an important resource, and is of the essence when hunting mature bucks. How wisely we use it will ultimately be reflected in our bowhunting success. Evaluate seasons past and the time that was wasted, and the time that was not. Together, you'll find a better plan for your next hunt. Oh, and remember—there's one thing you can count on when you're chasing trophy whitetails—time will fly because you're having fun!

20

The Rattler's Almanac

By Gary Clancy
(October 2000)

The first buck that ever responded to the clatter of my rattling horns is forever etched in my mind. What I felt when that buck came hurrying through the timber, looking for the fight, was pure excitement. Until that moment, I did not really know if rattling would work. I had heard a little about it and read some things, but nobody I knew had ever actually rattled in a buck. I remember thinking, "Wow, this stuff really does work!"

Since that morning, I've been fortunate to travel extensively in the pursuit of my favorite big-game animal. Wherever I go, my horns or some other rattling device are with me. I've had bucks come to rattling in gobs of states and provinces, and while I have gotten over the "wow," the adrenaline rush that jolts me when a buck comes to the horns is still there.

Thus, I find it sad that most whitetail hunters have never rattled in a buck. Many have tried, become discouraged, and thrown in the towel.

Rattling can work anywhere, so long as the doe to buck ratio is in balance.
Credit: Gary Clancy

Others have not even tried. Most are convinced that rattling is something that only works on the exclusive ranches of South Texas. When I give seminars on rattling, no matter what part of the country, the most frequent comment I hear is that "Rattlin' don't work around here!"

With that attitude, these hunters are right. Rattling never will work for them. But after several decades of horn shaking across North America, I am convinced that rattling can work wherever whitetails exist.

Location

In real estate, location is everything. Many hunters believe that location is also the key to rattling success. If you're hunting a ranch in South Texas, or the deep forest of northern Saskatchewan, then rattling might just work, these hunters figure. But in Missouri, Alabama, New York, New Jersey, Wisconsin, or Pennsylvania, for example, forget it.

The truth is that location has nothing to do with rattling success. A Southern buck is as susceptible to rattling as a northern buck, and a buck in

The author with a monster he took while rattling. *Credit: Gary Clancy*

the east is just as likely to come to the horns as a western prairie whitetail. Nope; latitude and longitude have nothing to do with it. But the buck-to-doe ratio sure as heck does.

Buck-to-Doe Ratio

The reason why South Texas has developed a reputation as the horn-shaking mecca of the world is because 99.9 percent of the whitetail habitat is privately owned, the bulk of it as large ranches. Whitetails are managed as a cash crop on many of these ranches. Each mature buck is worth "X" dollars. Hunters of means pay big bucks for a chance at a big buck. To ensure that the land is carrying the optimum number of mature bucks, the deer herds are intensely managed to keep the buck-to-doe ratio as close to one-to-one as possible. Of course, achieving such a perfect balance is nearly impossible, but ratios of one-to-two or one-to-three are common on these ranches.

When a whitetail herd is comprised of one adult buck for every two or three adult does, there is going to be competition between the bucks for breeding rights. Any time there's competition between bucks, rattling is a very effective technique. If the buck-to-doe ratio is out of whack, as it is in many parts of the country today, there is little or no competition between bucks for breeding rights because every buck has all of the does he can handle and then some.

Competition and Curiosity

I look forward to the few opportunities I have to hunt in places where the buck-to-doe ratio is low enough to guarantee competition between mature bucks. But most of the seventy to ninety days I spend hunting deer each season are in places where the buck-to-doe ratio tips heavily in favor of the does. Yet, I have rattled in bucks in many of these less-than-ideal locations. Why? Whitetails are curious critters. When a buck hears what he believes to be two bucks fighting, pure curiosity will sometimes trip his trigger. This also explains why it is not uncommon for does to investigate the sound of rattling.

Perfect Timing

Timing is critical when it comes to rattling success. Sure, you might rattle in a buck anytime during the season, but your odds shoot way up when you present your case during the period when bucks are most likely to respond to your invitation. The exact dates vary by region and somewhat from year to year, but the prime period for rattling action is that ten-day to two-week stretch leading to the first wave of does entering estrus. This is when bucks are gearing up for the main event. Bucks are now on their feet for most of the day as they paw out scrapes, make rubs, and roam from doe group to doe group.

At the beginning of this period, most bucks that respond to the horns will come in slow and wary. But during those last frantic days, when a buck is beside himself with pent-up frustration, I've seen them literally charge in to the scene. It is quite unnerving to see a mature buck come crashing through the brush and skid to a halt right in front of you.

Success with the horns tapers off quickly once serious numbers of does come into estrus. In fact, in areas where does far outnumber bucks, rattling now is pretty much a waste of effort. But in regions where there is still some competition between bucks for available does, you can enjoy good success by continuing to rattle right through the breeding phase of the rut and into the first week or so of post-rut.

Thick or Thin?

Some horn-shakers say that you should always set up to rattle in heavy cover where a buck will feel most secure coming all the way. Other hunters claim that hunting relatively open habitat, where you can see a buck coming from a distance, is the ideal situation. Who is right? In my experience, both camps are right.

When bowhunting, I need that buck within thirty yards or less. So I rattle in heavy cover (unless I'm using a deer decoy). I choose heavy cover when rattling while bowhunting because a buck does not expect to see the bucks he hears fighting until he is right on top of them in heavy cover—so he is less likely to hang up. The problem with heavy cover is that bucks have this irritating habit of circling in downwind before committing themselves. To remedy this, set up with a large opening, river, steep bank, or something else at your back that deer will be reluctant to cross. This will encourage them to circle in front of you.

If you use a decoy while bowhunting, forget everything I just said about heavy cover. A decoy should be in the open where the deer can see it. When I'm gun hunting and can reach out there and touch them at 100 yards or more, I let them hang up! Let your weapon determine the cover from which you do your rattling.

You Can't Go Wrong

There is not a correct way to rattle. No two buck fights sound the same, so it is not important how you choose to work your rattling antlers. On the ground, many hunters like to rake brush and pound the ground while working the horns. Other hunters grunt, either by mouth or with a call, while they rattle. The truth is, you can make all of the racket you can muster and you will still never be able to duplicate the sounds two mature bucks make when they are really getting it on.

Most hunters don't rattle long enough. Keep sequences going for at least a minute or two. Give that buck time to make up his mind and then make the trip. And do more grinding than slamming. Whitetails do not butt heads like bighorn rams on that old Dodge truck commercial. Instead, they come together and grind and twist, trying to throw their opponent off balance.

Real or Fake?

I've used just about every rattling device on the market. I'm convinced that when the time is right and the buck is in the mood, what you rattle with makes no difference. That buck is coming! I've had a number of bucks come to the sound of the bell on my dog's collar, and I know guys who have rattled in bucks by clattering a couple of aluminum arrows together when they forgot their rattling antlers.

I prefer a real set of antlers to anything else. I've used my rattling antlers a long time, and I've got faith in them. They feel right in my hands, like my favorite bow or hunting knife. And nothing sounds as much like

When rattling, set up so you can see the area downwind of your location, as that's where big bucks usually appear. *Credit: Gary Clancy*

the real thing as the real thing does, but I don't think that authenticity counts for much with the deer.

I've always got something I can use to rattle. During peak rattling periods, I usually carry my rattling horns, but at other times of the year, you won't find me without a rattling bag or other rattling device like those made by Lohman or M.A.D. in my fanny pack. Many times I have rattled in deer, when I had no intention of doing any rattling that day. I could not have done that if I had not been in the habit of carrying some type of rattling device with me on every trip to the woods.

When calling on windy days, or when you really need distance, plastic calls have a big edge over real horns, bags or fake antlers.

Tie Them Up

When hunting from a treestand, tie your rattling antlers to your pull rope after you are settled in your stand. If you're working the horns and a buck comes in and catches you with them in your hands (this is the voice of experience talking), you can pitch the antlers to the ground and grab your gun or bow. Another neat thing about this trick is that if the buck hangs up out of range or behind some cover, just jiggle the rope and the antlers will clatter together at the base of your tree. Not only will this encourage the buck to come on in, but his focus is also on the ground instead of up in the air.

Not only does rattling work, but rattling in a buck is a whole lot of fun. Make it one of your new century resolutions to give rattling an honest attempt.

For subscription information to *Buckmasters Whitetail Magazine,* contact: Buckmasters, Ltd., Attn: Customer Service, 10350 Highway 80 East, Montgomery, AL 36117; or visit Buckmasters.com.